Advance Praise for the Book

'The focus of the book—single moms in India transforming themselves to overcome so many challenges—is wonderful. The stories are compelling and will surely inspire many women.'

—Dr Patricia J. Crane
Author, speaker, trainer, and co-founder of
Heart Inspired Presentations

'Heartbreaking, brutal, too honest, but infused with a ray of hope that nothing is impossible when the true spirit of womanhood emerges from the veils of ambiguity. A reference guide to any woman seeking healing from within.'

—Dr C. S. Chandrika
Author, columnist, and women's rights activist

'An honest depiction of what a section of women undergoes in our society. I say that this book is not just for single moms; it's a book which we men need to read, and our sons need to read, so that each of us can introspect ourselves before entering into relationships. A real eye-opener.'

—P. J. Joshua
Chief editor, *Malayala Manorama*

'The real stories of single women and their healing as shared in this book by Dr Haseena inform us that women are brave warriors. This book must be read widely, not only by women but also men, to enable them to understand and change.'

—Abha Iyengar
Poet, editor, and mentor

'Brimming with wisdom and imparting transformative insights, this is a compelling read for anyone wanting to grow and evolve.'

—Dr G. L. Sampoorna
Psychologist, Heal Your Life® India teacher-trainer,
and founder of Rathna Centre of Conscious Living

'A book that helps you understand the unsaid and unheard trials and tribulations that every woman goes through. Truly a poignant and emotional read!'

—V. M. Ibrahim
Editor, *Madhyamam*

'*The Kintsugi Moms* is a treasure each of us needs to hold close to our hearts. Every word shared in this book is a blessing, allowing deep reflection. Thank you, Haseena, for being the gift you are to the world.'

—Babbu Lakhvinder Gill
Heal Your Life® worldwide teacher-trainer at
Heart Inspired Presentations

The
Kintsugi
Moms

Transformative Insights from a Healer's Diary

Dr Haseena Chokkiyil

Hay House Publishers India

Australia • India
United Kingdom • United States

Hay House Publishers (India) Pvt. Ltd.
Muskaan Complex, Plot No.3, B-2 Vasant Kunj, New Delhi-110 070, India
Hay House Inc., PO Box 5100, Carlsbad, CA 92018-5100, USA
Hay House UK, Ltd., The Sixth Floor, Watson House, 54 Baker Street, W1U 7BU, UK
Hay House Australia Pty Ltd., 18/36 Ralph St., Alexandria NSW 2015, Australia

Email: contact@hayhouse.co.in
www.hayhouse.co.in

ISBN 978-93-94613-00-3
ISBN 978-93-94613-01-0 (e-book)

Dedicated to
Fayaz—my son, best friend, and partner in crime.

Contents

Foreword

*W*hen Dr Haseena reached out to me with her book, *The Kintsugi Moms*, an anthology of stories of women exploring different facets of motherhood, healing, and empowerment, I felt instantly connected. Being a mother is tough. It is complicated, messy, and chaotic at times. But it also is immensely beautiful and very human at heart. Choosing to be a single mom is even more challenging and a title not so many women adorn by choice.

I am proud to be a single mom by personal choice, answering to a call from my soul. But the real-life characters in Haseena's book are in this role by some play of destiny, where they are forced to get separated from their partners and choose to shoulder the responsibility of bringing up their children single-handedly. These warrior moms have invariably gone through a broken phase from which they have beautifully fixed themselves to the extent that they are all celebrating their sojourns on earth with so much gratification and peace.

I believe that every woman has a story. A story that celebrates the myriad journeys we undertake—the physical transformations of our bodies and the inner pathways of our emotional lives. To truly celebrate a woman, we must accept all the nuanced differences and immense vulnerability that gives her strength. The stories of the women Haseena has helped to heal showcase that vulnerability and resilience. She has helped them to transform the broken pieces of themselves, their losses, their grief, and their pain into works of art. Her role as a holistic healer in each of their lives fascinated me. It was new knowledge to me that homoeopathy, an alternative system of medicine, has immense possibilities in the radical cure of many chronic diseases.

Dr Haseena told me about her battle with adrenal insufficiency, which again struck a chord. In 2014, when I was diagnosed with the same, I had no more fight left in me but was not ready to give up. I decided to fight anyway and started to strengthen my mind-body connection with nunchaku meditation and yoga. With sustained efforts, I recovered and my adrenal glands started to produce cortisol again. My healing was in some ways a miracle. I still remember my doctor from Cleveland clinic calling to tell me that in thirty-five plus years of his practice, he had never seen an instance where the body started producing cortisol again. From being told that I needed to take steroids for the rest of my life, I was free to live my life and nurture myself and my soul in the ways I wanted to. It made me see that the pain was just as worthy as the joy of transmuting that suffering into healing. That long, dark period in my life was a wake-up call—it made me cherish my body more, and I realised that healing really begins from within.

When Dr Haseena said that she took inspiration from my story to heal herself, I felt really glad. I realised that there are many women who drew courage and inspiration from my story. So, when she requested that I write the foreword for her book, I was more than happy to consent. Being a single mom herself, having transcended a plethora of challenges, both physical and emotional, and equipped with the right tools of holistic healing, I feel that she has chosen the most apt niche to embark upon her debut attempt as a writer.

We are all warriors, often battling with ourselves, others, or with life's circumstances. But let me tell you that with courage, positivity, love, and compassion, we can win those battles and heal ourselves provided we have the right guidance and mentoring. That's what Dr Haseena's stories reflect.

I wish her all success in her endeavour and hope that millions of women get inspiration from this chronicle of diverse experiences and final victory of women, so rightfully coined *The Kintsugi Moms*.

—Sushmita Sen
Former Miss Universe, Bollywood actress, poet,
and a proud mother

Preface

$\mathcal{B}$roken clouds shower down as rain. Broken and upturned soil sets as fields. Broken crops yield seeds. Broken seeds yield new crops. Have you noticed how beautifully the universe uses broken things? Have you noticed that everything that is broken yearns for a new life? A broken piece of china at the disposal of an expert artisan becomes even more beautiful, stronger, and resilient than before.

What if this broken vessel is your own life? What if the cracks on it represent a part of your personal history? How would it feel if you are endowed with the art and means to repair those cracks to become a stronger version of yourself?

The word I choose to describe such a life is *kintsugi*, the ancient Japanese art of mending and fixing broken pieces of pottery with gold and lacquer, thus accentuating its cracks rather than hiding them. It has its metaphor which is much deeper: that by embracing the damage, the broken object accepts its past and paradoxically becomes more robust, beautiful, and precious than before.

***

As I sit down to write this book, I am filled with the immense satisfaction of having been granted the opportunity to so beautifully mend the cracks that life inflicted on me and the many women I have encountered as a holistic healer.

Womanhood is in itself a roller coaster of adventures; some are beautiful while others are challenging and devastating. One such challenge, which resonates deeply with me, is the state of women who choose to raise their children single-handedly after separating from their partners, either due to death or divorce. According to a United Nations study on the progress of women in 2019-20, it is estimated that about 4.5 per cent of households in India are run by single mothers which amounts to a staggering forty million figure. A global study, with data from eighty-nine countries, shows that out of all the lone parent households, single mothers head eighty-four per cent of them, translating to a whopping 101.3 million. The challenges of these women are not properly addressed by the world at large and mostly overlooked.

***

OMG! I AM A SINGLE MOM NOW! One fine day, she wakes up to the new reality of her life, bringing with it a mixture of unprecedented feelings and unforeseen challenges. Most of all, there is a sense of determination to forge ahead, for the sake of the little soul/s dependent on her.

Any experienced single mom will endorse that being one is never a bed of roses. Though it brings immense joy and satisfaction on one side, the title comes with a whole lot of added responsibilities as compared to mothers doing the same in the shade of a supportive family setup. She has the inescapable duty of catering to all the needs of her children. She has to be the pillar of strength and support to them and be more vigilant than her counterparts in wedlock. As the children grow up, she also has to cater to their doubts and anxieties about marriage and relationships and handle them delicately yet strongly so that their convictions about life are built upon the right foundation.

The fact is that single parenting takes bravery, resilience, and fortitude. Regardless of whether you are leaving a partnership after abuse or being widowed, it is critical to address past pain and work on healing the wounds the separation might have created. Even if single by choice, you need to work on yourself.

Because amidst the rat race to raise the children unscathed and whole, without the support of a partner, a single mother is left with an array of psychological and physical challenges requiring deep healing and revival as she readily compromises the most important person in her life: *herself!* Usually, it is seen that once she learns to work on herself and is reconciled to the fact that she can become the epitome of inner strength, her child turns out to be more grounded and stronger than a normal family-bred child. On the other hand, if she underplays herself and cannot rise above the victim-consciousness and succumbs to the atrocities of society, her child imbibes the negative vibes and may repeat the same patterns in his/her relationships and outlooks.

Therefore, it is not only necessary but inevitable that once you have adorned the title of single motherhood, you strive to repair and elevate yourself to such heights of confidence and peace that your child looks up to you as the most trustworthy guide, role model, and teacher of life lessons. As the anchor of your family, it's especially important that you find a way to parenting with joy and confidence.

This book is an offering to every single mother who has stood at the threshold of utter helplessness, insecurity, and confusion, gone through personal conflicts and healing crises, and finally learnt to empower herself to celebrate motherhood and womanhood in their full glory. It is an inquiry into her emotional, mental, physical, sexual, and spiritual realms and the up and down trajectories on which life took her along to reach her ultimate purpose in life.

As I observe from a statistical point of view, it is seen that almost all stories have a common thread. All single mothers have gone through a broken phase from which they pulled themselves together for a purpose much higher than their perceptions. They have faced the judgements and sinister outlooks of conventional society before finally reaching a point of realisation that salvation and satisfaction in life is an inside job and that they need not conform to extrinsic opinions or beliefs.

Since my clients are mostly Indian, I get to see their lives at close quarters as compared to the lives of their Western counterparts. I make an apology if my views are a wee bit short-sighted or prejudiced but from the extensive observations and interviews conducted in the course of writing this book, I am tempted to conclude that the essential needs and challenges of these warrior moms are more or less the same, irrespective of country, race, or religion.

I met many of these women when they had only darkness for company and travelled alongside each of them in their journey towards healing and self-discovery, playing different roles: as a homoeopathic physician, psychological counsellor, nutritionist, wellness coach, and on some occasions, just as a witness or silent listener.

Many of these healed women have been fortunate to find happiness in another marriage/relationship. Some have carved envious places for themselves in the entrepreneurial sphere while others have recognised that their sense of fulfilment lies in social service. All of them are but goddesses who have surpassed the tests of destiny and that is why I like to call these remoulded women—the kintsugi moms.

I would like to state here that whether simple or complex, none of the tools mentioned in this book are my inventions. I arrived at these methods through books and broadminded, selfless guides and mentors who were simply ready to share their knowledge for the betterment and redemption of wider humanity. All those gods in human guise are founts of knowledge of which I am but a humble channel. At this point, I would also like to state that the strategies I advance in this book for survival and healing are not limited to single mothers. They are for anybody going through a healing crisis in any area of existence. It is just a sheer play of serendipity that the women in this chronicle happen to be single moms.

I began my career as a homoeopathic physician under a great teacher, Dr Ajay Kumar Babu, who demonstrated the efficacy of the Hahnemannian principles of homoeopathy in the radical cure of a vast majority of diseases stamped incurable by modern concepts of medicine. From then on, destiny has taken so many tumultuous somersaults, taking me deeper into the various aspects of healing through a myriad of epiphanies and that is how books became my constant companions and teachers of life lessons. After my first self-help book by Louise L. Hay, which I read when I was facing my first healing crisis—the initial stage of cancer in my uterus—many authors entered my life as beacons of light, leaving me in absolute awe of the bounty of the universe. Each little tip I offer in this book has been carved out from my twenty-seven years of experience as a healer and from my own personal challenges.

It is my firm conviction that this book did not come into your preview by accident. I am sure that after witnessing the stories outlined here, the memories that you fear and have rendered you powerless to pick up the broken pieces of your life will turn into your advantage. They will enable you to become the adhesive gold to join the broken pieces of yourself together and emerge as the most beautiful kintsugied version of yourself.

'Out of suffering have emerged the strongest of souls;
the most massive characters are seared with scars.'
—Kahlil Gibran

Introduction

My dear reader, before you delve in, let me give an overview of what to expect while flipping through the pages of this humble attempt.

Each chapter begins with the story of one woman, followed by the strategies adopted to heal her. Only one tool is discussed in each chapter. Invariably, all the stories are painful to begin with and may disturb you to the core. I have received suggestions to cut short the tales of woe and concentrate on the healing modules. However, I find it prudent to stick to this style of presentation in order to shed light on the volume and diversity of challenges women face in different life situations across the globe. They will resonate with you and give you that ray of hope to overcome any challenge in life. You can take immense inspiration from the ways they put themselves together even after all that life had meted out to them. And if the stories still traumatise you, I request you to understand that they are our sisters who need our unstinted spiritual support and validation. The healing techniques I have advocated were always there in the universe and you can access them from any of the sources I have referred to throughout the book. But the insights from each of the traumas and challenges of these women are unique and a guiding light to anyone facing similar situations in their lives.

After the eight stories of survival, the last two chapters are the ultimate takeaways for the reader. It is the consolidation and summary of all the healing modules I have used in each of the chapters. They are dealt with in simple, layman's language.

All medical and metaphysical terms are accompanied with their clarifications. The closing chapter, the Epilogue, deals with my serendipitous journey as a healer and a woman who has gone through a kintsugi process myself to be an authentic advocate of the tools I so confidently put forward to the world.

You might be wondering about the Japanese words used in the titles of the chapters. Please don't be baffled, my dear. The meanings are explained in the subheadings. Most of these words came to me through years of reading every piece of literature that came my way. The Japanese way of life and their philosophy have fascinated the whole world for ages and maybe that is why so many of their words circulate in the literary world. I was simply drawn towards them when selecting the titles and it was neither deliberate nor intentional.

Thank you for picking up this book and I hope that you see the light at the end of whatever tunnel you are going through after reading it. Now, let's travel with some incredible women through their labyrinths of experiences and get the nuances of their healing journeys.

PS: The names, locations, and life situations of the protagonists have been changed to maintain confidentiality.

SECTION 1

Chapter 1

ARIGATO

(Gratitude - The Game Changer)

There was an undeniable inner prodding to start with the story of Ayesha, the latest bead in the chain of my kintsugi moms. The initial tool I employed to heal her was the very first one that transformed my mindset forever, an interesting coincidence which I believe was by no means accidental but rather a clear sign from the divine.

Our first meeting was over a Whatsapp video call at the beginning of the Covid-19 lockdown period. When Ayesha appeared onscreen with a carelessly worn head veil, unkempt hair, face devoid of any make-up, and lack of confidence writ large in her fidgety body language, my first impression was that of a shy, orthodox, and uneducated Muslim lady. I prepared myself to bow to her level of understanding and asked in a very complacent tone, '*As-salamu alaykum*, Ayesha. What can I do for you?'

'Doctor, I haven't slept for the past two years. I am completely aware of what is happening around me even if I manage to doze off for an hour or two. I just want to sleep soundly every night,' she replied in a meek voice, finding it difficult to even look directly at the camera.

'What do you feel when you try to sleep?' I asked.

'I get a lot of disturbing thoughts, doc. I lost my father and mother, whom I was close to and dependent on, in the last two years. I feel lonely and frightened when I close my eyes and I see the scary episodes of my life like a screenplay. I dare not shut my eyes.' Her voice trailed off as tears started rolling down.

I allowed them to flow unstinted for a while and then inquired, 'Are you alone? I understand that you have three kids from the introduction message you sent me.'

'Yes, three girls. One is completing her final year in dentistry, one is doing her graduation in aeronautical engineering, and the youngest one is finishing school,' her face lit up with pride while replying.

I was flabbergasted. A single, uneducated mother guiding her children to such premier levels of education!

'They stay in hostels and I live alone in a rented apartment. The apartment is secure, but I am scared to lie down alone at night. I hear voices and see my dead parents and weep for hours,' she continued.

'How do you spend your days?' I enquired further.

'Well, I run a software shop and I am engaged till evening. It is the rest of the day and night that are unbearable. I am the president of the ladies wing of a local political party and I regularly visit a palliative care centre, but lately, I shy away from all social activities,' she said in a matter-of-fact tone.

I had judged the book by its cover! I sat open-mouthed for a few seconds and made no pretension of hiding my surprise. 'Ayesha, from the way you have presented yourself, I took you for a woman with no resources. Just a helpless, uneducated single mother, a victim of domestic abuse,' I admitted.

For the first time, an amused smile crossed the sad face. 'Yes, ma'am, I sure am a victim, but I am a postgraduate in Arabic studies. I was the chairperson in the college union and a dedicated social activist, but now I have lost interest in everything. I find it hard to mingle with people. My life revolves around my shop and home.'

My goodness gracious! Here was a woman of substance reduced to a vegetable-like existence by the stresses of life. Her condition could be easily diagnosed by professionals like me as a case of post-traumatic stress disorder and secondary depression, but what was the way out? No matter the solution, one thing was sure; it would be a gruelling journey through many modalities of healing, each of which would require multiple sessions.

I sharpened my physician skills to dive into her inner recesses, to understand the workings of her mind and physique, to comprehend the exact nature of her emotional status and coping mechanisms. Here is her heart-wrenching story without a pinch of exaggeration.

As mentioned earlier, Ayesha was a versatile student, orator, and social activist with ample family support. But in that patriarchal society, when it came to marriage, a middle-class Muslim girl had no say whatsoever. She was married off to an 'eligible bachelor' working in Dubai who gave her three children apart from a heavy dose of verbal and physical abuse in the next twelve years after which she finally summed up the courage to leave him for good. But the years of torture left their indelible scars on her psyche. Not to mention the accompanying physical ailments-diabetes, hypertension, migraine, and sleeplessness.

As I interrogated further, I understood that the emotion ruling her was grief. Insecurity, anxiety, and resentment were all there but the most predominant emotion was grief. After losing her parents unexpectedly one after the other in a short interval of time and with her children on their own highways to life, she felt absolutely lost. I noted the first important symptom (grief) and got ready for the remaining story.

'Tell me about your childhood and marriage, Ayesha,' I prodded. The next half hour was like going through a tragic movie script.

***

Though from a remote village, her father, who was a local political leader, encouraged her to pursue studies and learn to make a living. When the aforesaid marriage proposal came, she was assured that she would be allowed to complete her postgraduation and would be taken to Dubai. The groom was apparently a company supervisor with the provision for a family visa. But the big story of deception unveiled itself on the second day of the wedding. This was his second marriage and he already had a child. Also, he was just a car driver who blatantly confessed that he married for money alone. Ayesha's jewellery was taken away in the very first week itself. Her postgraduation dreams were thwarted right at the onset as she tried to merge with the new family which was in stark contrast to hers. It was a joint family of fourteen members along with five cows and several hens. A typical day for Ayesha began at 4:30 a.m. and ended far past midnight. Harassments from a vindictive mother-in-law and grandmother-in-law further added to her miseries.

The so-called husband flew to the Middle East in a matter of two weeks after marriage. Nine months later, Ayesha held a baby girl with no support whatsoever for infant care. He returned home two years later only to give her another baby girl. She had no guts to stand up for herself and tolerated the beast, even in bed, like a smothered butterfly. After the birth of her third daughter and the deaths of her abusive mothers-in-law, it was the father-in-law's turn to torture her. On one fateful day when no one was at home, he tried to molest her while she was working in the kitchen. Somehow, this breach of dignity ignited the warrior in her. She screeched and seethed with rage, yelling at him to back off or else she would bring in the whole neighbourhood. He was taken aback for a few seconds by her bold reaction but threatened to kill her if she uttered even a single word about the incident.

For the first time, Ayesha found her voice and reported this to her husband. He flew down for a detailed family discussion but ultimately the whole story was painted in an entirely different hue. It turned out that it was Ayesha who had approached her father-in-law. She was stamped as an immoral, sex-starved lady in front of the whole crowd. She stood shocked at the turn of events; attacked, accused, and verbally humiliated by everyone alike, yet was unable to utter a single word in self-defence. How could she reveal this to her parents? Such a demeaning accusation with no evidence to substantiate her innocence!

She went on living like a machine, tolerating every vindictive comment and physical torture. Until one day, her husband knocked her down near the kitchen sink with a heavy blow at the back of her head. As she lay on the floor, bewildered and bleeding heavily, she saw her youngest daughter screaming and hitting her father with a broom, the last image before a complete blackout. After days in the hospital and out of the coma, she finally found the grit to take matters into her hands. The memory of her little girl's ferocious yet helpless face gave her the much-needed push to act. She spoke to her father, who immediately sprang into action and filed a case. He shifted her to a rented apartment with the three girls and coaxed her to complete her postgraduation and acquire a diploma in computers.

Slowly, Ayesha picked up the threads of life and started earning enough to sustain the family. The old spark of leadership emerged once again and she brought up the daughters to be immensely strong and gave them the best of education. She felt stronger than ever but still couldn't procure a legal divorce due to lack of evidence for domestic violence, from the court's point of view. She lived in constant horror of being attacked by her husband and in-laws. In between, she lost her parents who had been her biggest pillars of support. The post-traumatic stress was beyond her threshold and that was when she decided to reach out to me.

***

I sat silent for a while, absorbing and visualising the horrendous incidents in this woman's life. It was unbelievable that such an educated lady tolerated so much humiliation and abuse even at the cost of losing her life.

I asked out of sheer curiosity, 'Ayesha, why did you stay silent to all those injustices when you had a supportive family?'

Her answer was so typical. 'I didn't want my parents to panic hearing my tale of woes. They had married me off with the best of intentions and toiled a lot to meet the dowry demands. Just when I was leaving home on the wedding day, my father called me aside and said, "Dear, you are entering into a new life where everything will be different. Don't ever complain or retaliate against your in-laws. See them as your own family and even if a rope is wound around your neck, find ways to escape it but never ever talk or do ill to your husband's family." Ayesha took his words as a mantra.

'Phew!' I exclaimed to myself. Even in these times of women empowerment and feminism, the mindsets of our women are still bound by the age-old norms of reverence and obedience to culture. The victim consciousness still sticks on like an irremovable stamp on our women. Unbelievable! But this is a simple cut-out of the reality existing in Indian culture even today. My speculations were useless at this point. My primary duty was to help her sleep and move on in life. 'Or is that all?' I asked myself. 'No,' was the emphatic answer.

Once a broken vessel like this comes to me, it is my mission to ensure that she gets completely healed so that she can discover her hidden strengths and launch upon her journey of self-realisation and final victory. I would have to do immense healing work in multiple sessions to peel off each negative layer and bring out the shining diamond in her. I had to take one small step at a time to finally enable Ayesha to take the reins of life back in her hands.

Initially, I dived into my homoeopathic side and emerged with a medicine that covered all her mental patterns. Ignatia was my drug of choice. (Ignatia is given to people suffering from post-traumatic stress, especially due to the loss of loved ones, which, if not properly addressed, can upset the balance of the hormones and neurotransmitters in the body. This can lead to many psychosomatic disorders like migraine, hypertension, ulcers, and inflammation of all sorts. For more information, visit: www.materiamedica.info/en/materia-medica/james-tyler-kent/ignatia).

No self-healing techniques could be advised at this stage as her mind was clouded with the dark veil of depression. I explained to her that I was trying to balance her brain so that she would feel calm and peaceful, and insisted the need for her full cooperation and discipline in continuing the processes that I would be prescribing. She was more than willing to adhere.

'Doctor, will it help me sleep?' she asked with eyes gleaming with hope.

'Wait and watch, Ayesha. Believe in yourself and in me, your mentor for the time being. And of course, in the power of the universal intelligence which has connected us for this interlude. Start the medicine today. Three days later I want you to begin with one small routine that you may find silly or mundane at the onset. Nevertheless, continue without questioning,' I told.

'What is it, doctor?' she inquired with a childlike curiosity that warmed my heart.

I explained, 'I want you to start writing a journal. Take a small book, laptop, or even your phone. But I would prefer you to use the traditional pen and paper. Write down everything in your mind without interrupting the flow. Write your joys and sorrows, the aha moments, and also those heart-breaking moments, like a small autobiography. Don't read or rewrite it. Just leave it at that.' I continued,

'Then take a fresh page every day. Spend five to ten minutes finding at least ten things you are grateful for in life. It can be anything, like the food you had, the blessing of a shelter, or your children. Say "thank you" three times after writing each of your blessings. Continue it for the next twenty-eight days without interruption. If you forget to write down an entry at any point, revert to three days and continue. Just go about it and don't question the process. After writing ten things that you already have in life, write three things that you want to manifest in your life. Be it money or happiness, to sleep peacefully, or anything that you simply crave. Just feel the joy of having it in your life, visualise it, and say "thank you" as if you have already received it.'

She looked perplexed at my seemingly ridiculous suggestions. 'Just do it without thinking much, dear. I will explain the metaphysical science behind the process once you do it for a week. Enjoy it like a kid introduced to the first nursery rhyme and update me in a week.'

She called me after the third day, brimming with joy. 'Doctor, I slept deeply for five hours straight, wrote three poems after years, and also nineteen pages of my life's story. I am overjoyed. Thank you.'

I was also overjoyed and grateful to her for allowing me to be a channel for her return journey into wholeness. However, years of experience had taught me that it was just an initial enthusiasm and lasting results were yet to come. Ignatia had acted wonderfully, but the radical change had to come from her sustained effort and adherence to the process. I reassured her about the efficacy and accuracy of the exercise and encouraged her to start with gratitude journaling.

A week later, she reported better energy levels and creativity, but sleep eluded her once again. It was something I had been expecting. I asked her to go deeper into the gratitude exercise and start forgiving and releasing everything and everyone from her past.

The very next week, Ayesha sent me a voice message at 6:30 a.m. She sounded very happy and enthusiastic. 'Doctor, I slept for seven hours at a stretch. I missed two *namaz* (Muslim prayer ritual done five times a day), but I am overflowing with energy and peace. Thank you so much.'

I knew that Ayesha was on the road to recovery. All she needed was regular guidance.

Three months later, she called me with a handful of unexpected achievements. Her daughter's marriage had been fixed and due to the Covid lockdown, the expenses for the ceremony were cut short. Her second daughter had got into The Indian Institute of Technology—the most prestigious institute in the country—to pursue her master's degree. She was able to sell her land to a bidder who appeared all of a sudden and therefore the tuition fees were taken care of. Ayesha also joined a yoga class and started a hub to help single women entrepreneurs to find their niche. Above all, she was sleeping for six hours at night with no medicines at all.

After hearing her achievements, I could only say *arigato* to the universe and Rhonda Byrne who introduced me to this wonderful tool of gratitude journaling. And, of course, arigato to the master of homoeopathy, Dr Samuel Hahnemann, and my mentor, Dr Ajay Kumar Babu. Just one healing tool and two doses of ignatia had done so much for a soul groping in darkness.

What I initiated in Ayesha was no miracle healing. She was just introduced to time-tested and proven processes already set forth by brilliant souls. The ultimate goal was to reprogram her subconscious mind and thought patterns. The kintsugi process had to start from her side, which she accomplished with stoic resolve and perseverance.

In due course, she attended my online workshops based on the philosophy of Louise L. Hay, the great metaphysical teacher whose healing tools are internationally acclaimed. By the end of six months, she sent me a picture of herself receiving an award for being 'The Best Woman Influencer' in her district. She had won the award for training five hundred economically backward women to use computers. She shared another picture of her speaking about women empowerment on a dais adorned with a member of parliament. She had also started her own charitable institution to train financially and educationally backward women in computers and had already trained over seven hundred women by then.

There was no end to the joy and satisfaction I got witnessing her victories and that too in such a short span of time. The perks of being in a vocation you are truly passionate about!

Gratitude Journaling

The Quran says: 'And (remember) if you are grateful I will give you more, but if you are ungrateful, verily my punishment is indeed severe.'

The Gospel says: 'Whoever has gratitude will be given more, and he will have abundance. Whoever does not have gratitude, even what he has will be taken from him.'

This simple rule of being grateful for what you have and you will attract more instances to be grateful for operates through the universal law that governs all lives. It is actually nothing but a tool to exhort the law of attraction into play. Meaning, whatever you think and feel, you will attract it. So, when you are in the energy of gratitude, you create a resonant frequency to attract things and circumstances that matches that frequency. Similarly, the more you think about the lack in your life, the more lack you attract.

If you make it a conscious habit to always create positive thoughts and actions, then experiences of a similar wavelength will be attracted to you. Gratitude journaling is one of the best tools to rewire your brain from negativity to positivity, thus attracting all that you really crave in life.

From the physiological point of view, it can be explained as follows: whatever we consistently think becomes like a GPS for our brain. Each word we think or say to ourselves has a frequency and energy that the brain instantly recognises. The brain produces corresponding chemicals which are released into our body through neural pathways and that changes the alchemy of our body, thus making us happy, positive, and joyful or anxious and negative, depending on the type of thoughts. This is called the reticular activating system.

The gratitude journal and twenty-eight days ritual have been adapted from the book, *The Magic*, written by Rhonda Byrne, which has transformed millions of lives, including mine. I felt like a fool when I first practised it years ago. After manifesting the desired car and overcoming health crises and relationship issues, I realised the immense potential of this technique and tuned myself for only observing and receiving what was best for me. It was like I held the key to my destiny with just a simple shift of my focus from negativity to seeing everything from the perspective of gratitude. From then on, I have added it to my modules for healing. It has helped every single client of mine who diligently practised it.

A gratitude journal is, quite simply, a tool to keep track of the good things in life. No matter how difficult and defeating life can sometimes feel, there is always something to feel grateful for. A lot of research has been done on this topic and the results are invariably encouraging.

- Gratitude journaling has been shown to help divorced parents forgive their ex-spouse(s), an extremely important step towards positive co-parenting (Rye, Fleri, Moore, Worthington, Wade, Sandage, and Cook, 2012).
- A study of a three-month trial of gratitude journaling found that both finding things to be grateful for

and expressing your gratitude have a significant and positive impact on well-being and depression (O'Connell, O'Shea, and Gallagher, 2017).

- Another study showed that Turkish freshmen who completed a three-week gratitude journal experienced greater gratitude, better adjustment, higher life satisfaction, and enhanced positive effect, compared to a control group of freshmen who did not complete a gratitude journal (Işık and Ergüner-Tekinalp, 2017).

So, it is evident that gratitude journaling seems to have a lot of potential upsides and no noticeable downsides. This beautiful exercise will be further elaborated in the chapter 'The Road Map to Kintsugi'.

Chapter 2

KENZEN

(Health - The Ultimate Wealth)

Vydehi, 36 years/Female, Height 160 cm, Weight 95 kg, Blood pressure 90/70 mm of hg, Pulse 65, Temp 98.6 °F. The duty nurse handed over the case sheet with the initial vital assessment and ushered in a lady looking about fifty years old. She was dark-faced (not dark-complexioned but pigmented), had a big stye over one eye, was obese, slow in gait, and wore a glum expression. To any experienced physician, the initial appearance was enough to conclude that she had a hormonal imbalance. As she slumped onto the visitor's chair, I took in the massive energy depletion and lack of life in her eyes. In spite of her sharp features and dove-like brown eyes, there was nothing attractive in her demeanour; she looked like a living corpse.

After the initial introduction, I looked at her empathetically and asked, 'What brings you here, Vydehi?'

She began her story. 'It started around five years ago, doctor, as occasional bouts of bleeding which would last for three or four days after the normal periods. Many opined that it could have been due to a slight change post-delivery and I ignored it for a few months. But it started getting heavier till it reached a stage where I bled for three to four weeks at a stretch.' She continued, 'I approached my gynaecologist who diagnosed it as endometrial hyperplasia and advised hormonal pills. However, the bleeding did not stop and I also started putting on weight.

This has continued for the last three years and now my doctor has diagnosed a big fibroid and that the only solution is the removal of the uterus. She says there is a precancerous lesion and if it is not removed, it is invariably heading to cancer. I am terrified of the disease, doctor! I am perpetually tired and weep at the slightest pretext. I feel like I cannot even carry myself through the day. I am anaemic but no amount of food is elevating my haemoglobin. My gynaecologist says that as long as this heavy bleeding lasts, my blood count will not improve. I also have been on medication for hypothyroidism for the last five years.' She finished off in one breath.

I was meticulously noting down every point. She had all the telltale symptoms of hypothyroidism—obesity, fatigue, lack of interest in daily activities, slowness in body movements, and inordinate mood fluctuations. She was sick, really sick. I enquired about similar issues with any of her family members. There were none.

'Okay, now tell me about your life. Where is your husband?' I probed further.

'Doctor, I am divorced. I have a six-year-old son and I am unemployed, living at the mercy of my parents. I am a graduate but have never ever gone out for a job.'

'Why?' I asked curiously.

The answer was a sigh and a sob. I let her weep for a while, neither interrupting nor comforting. As the sobs got feebler, she looked up with an apologetic smile and I offered the customary box of tissues. After picking one, she answered meekly, 'My husband wouldn't let me.'

Vydehi poured out her life story over the next twenty minutes. It was as if she was waiting for someone to ask about it.

***

It was a college love story that eventually ended in marriage. In fact, it was love at first sight and Vydehi won over the most sought-after boy on the campus. While girls vied to get even a glance of approval from him, it was Vydehi's beauty, smartness, and popularity that caught the attention of Mr Charming. They went on to date for a couple of years before deciding to get into wedlock amidst the disapproval of her family (since they were from different religious backgrounds). The initial months were straight out of a romantic movie. The couple clung to each other everywhere and did not even notice the passing by of days. She revelled in playing the multiple roles—of girlfriend, mother, sister, secretary, maid, and counsellor—for him. Her days began by touching his feet and catering to all his needs, in fact, only his needs. At night, she would finally throw herself on the bed for long escapades of sex even though she would be totally exhausted after the hectic day. He would shower her with praises for being his elixir of life and that was all she wanted to hear.

Time went by and with the added role of motherhood, the realities of life struck, and with them, came the monotony and hassles of matrimony. She thought of taking up a job to divert herself and also to bring in some added income. But her husband very tactfully convinced her to stay at home, saying he was earning enough and that their son needed her. She did not doubt his intentions one bit. As years passed, he soared to greater heights in his work, which soon brought with it new interests—alcohol and beautiful charming ladies who would give anything to enjoy his enigmatic personality. Vydehi was gradually pushed to the background. After the hectic days, the nights turned out to be mere physical acts of sex. The praises he used to shower upon her soon turned into body shaming and comments about her lack of efficiency. He began comparing her to his 'beautiful' work friends. With no family or financial support, being dismally insulted and abused sexually, and unable to express her needs either in bed or otherwise, she gradually crawled into her lonely niche of insecurity.

Eventually, she started reacting with bouts of weeping and complaining. That is when the real narcissist in him came out in all its fury. The ultimatum reached when he started bringing in ladies—his so-called business associates—to dinner and flirting openly in front of her. Vydehi was supposed to entertain them with good food and hospitality without a single word of protest.

One day, she returned home from an errand to find him in bed with a lady. She almost fainted at the sight and tried to stifle her cries with a tight grip on the mouth. He came out of the bedroom at that moment and even after knowing that she had seen it all, it did not perturb him a bit. He just ordered two teas and went in as if it was the most natural thing to do. That night, she could no longer hold herself back and reacted very violently. He, in turn, slapped her on the face and started accusing her instead. According to him, Vydehi was the sole person who had ruined his life by alluring him into an early marriage and he was forced to bring in more income to sustain their family. Whatever he did, including entertaining women, was part of the game to soar to greater heights in the profession, all for the sake of their family, and if she disapproved of his ways, she was free to leave. She stood confused, being the innocent naïve lady that she was. She literally believed that she was the culprit. Also, she could not leave him as she had neither family support whatsoever nor financial independence. He had taken care of that very well by making sure that she be nothing more than a slave to all his whims and fancies. However, she could no longer love him like before and started developing an aversion to sex and his company or proximity. Disagreements and fights became a common occurrence in the household and the helpless victim, their little son, had no other choice but to witness all the drama.

This continued for some time and ultimately, Vydehi had to take the drastic step when he started beating her up in front of their son. She didn't want the child to grow up in such a dismal environment. One fine day, she walked off from that life, though after being completely mutilated on all fronts. She went to her parents' home, but her father called her a cheat who went against all his expectations and asked her to leave the house. Had she been alone, she would have committed suicide then and there, but motherhood was something she couldn't deny and come what may, she had to live for her son. Therefore, she stuck on with her parents, bearing all the humiliation and insults.

Vydehi lived with no dreams and aspirations as she was sure that dreams never come true and plans never work. Lost, hurt, and new to the world of separation, she didn't know how to lead a life without her husband. Anger, sadness, fear, and insecurity were the only guests who would take turns and visit her, and whenever the intensity of these emotions went to the higher end, her drama would rise to its peak. She would scream, throw things, and at other times, go into long bouts of weeping. She was always in her own world, sometimes weeping, sometimes dreaming, or at other times, calling or messaging him shamelessly, just for a single moment of attention and love. She almost always had her eyes and ears glued to the front door of the house, waiting ardently to hear the horn of his car or see him walk through the door to just hold her tight and say reassuringly, 'Darling, I am back. I need only you. Let's start life anew.'

However, nothing of that sort happened. She stopped eating, exercising, and even bathing and changing her clothes. Her son was growing somewhere in the house, imbibing all the negativity. She got totally alienated from the outside world, until one day when she ended up scaring the little boy by showing the beast in her. During one of her maniac attacks, she hauled a big barrel of peanuts across the room. The little six-year-old was left aghast at the horrible sight. Nobody was at home and the helpless boy didn't know what to do except go from one corner to the other, picking up the scattered nuts like playing pick-up-sweets at a birthday party. She still remembers seeing from the corner of her eyes the distant look of fright and confusion on the chubby little face but not finding within her the mindset to comfort him. That night as she lay crying her heart out, she felt a silent vibration on the cot and impulsively reached out to where the little body was lying all curled up. To her utter dismay, there he was with tears running down his cheeks while trying to stifle his sobs with the end of the pillow stuffed into his mouth. Shocked, she gathered her little bundle and heartbreakingly asked, 'What's the matter, honey?'

To which came the helpless reply, 'I don't know, momma. I can't control my tears.'

Never had she wanted to hurt her son, but that day she had crossed all limits. She realised the damage her actions were doing to him. She got a jolt, a major one. She had hurt the feelings of the only person who brought an honest smile on her face, the only person who loved her unconditionally. What was more shocking was that a realisation that hadn't come for more than five years hit her in less than five minutes. It was the first time that she became aware of the damage that she had caused to her life in those years that she lost. It was almost like she had been unconscious for five years and had finally returned to reality, this time wide-awake and willing to take a step forward towards life.

***

'I want to live. I need to get cured for the sake of my son, doc.' Her plea was heart-wrenching. 'I heard about you from a friend. I came to know that you treat cancer and such incurable diseases with homoeopathic medicines and that you conduct sessions for mind-body healing. Hence, I thought I would try it out. Please help me, doctor,' she said, looking ardently into my eyes.

I could sense the helplessness of the lonely mother and really wanted to hand-hold her to wellness. However, being a holistic healer, I could not simply ask a few relevant questions, categorise her into one or two of the available medical diagnoses, give a medicine, and leave it at that. On the contrary, a client who enters my consultation room, in any broken condition, expects me to get at the crux of the problem and help eradicate it from her system once and for all. Vydehi expected more than the conventional protocols of treatment, which was only right, taking into consideration her choice of opting for me instead of a typical specialty-trained physician or surgeon.

Every time I encounter a patient like this, at least a couple of hours are guaranteed to be used for listening to their life history, diagnosing, and selecting the right holistic cure. An exhaustive interrogation into their personal history, starting right from their childhood to the point at which they are sitting in front of me, takes an immense amount of patience. They need to have a safe, trustworthy environment for catharsis. At the end of it, a clear picture emerges which culminates in a prolonged association of physician-patient relationship. It is an unambiguously accepted fact by both of us involved that this mutual journey is no child's play and complete adherence to the processes I suggest are complied with, leaving no space for personal irresponsibility.

The first step towards any journey of transformation must start with the body. A totally organised, peaceful, and healthy body is the foundation on which anything of significance can be built with lasting effects. A person who is physically sick and in pain cannot be asked to do meditation or exercises that involve the brain (For example, rewiring thought patterns and visualisations). It would be like asking a poor, hungry beggar at your doorstep to sing Hallelujah, while what he wants first is a stomach full of food. Hence, I aimed to revamp Vydehi's body first and help her cleanse it before going into any medical or metaphysical jargon. For that, I needed to find the right medical assistance in the form of homoeopathic medicines.

I confronted her, 'Vydehi, do you think that removing your uterus will take away the possibility of your contracting cancer?'

'I don't know doctor. I just don't want to die. I need to live for my son. That's all I know.' She looked lost.

'Well, then, I will have to educate you about the workings of our body and mind and actually what leads to cancer. You will also get an idea of how you get sick in the first place and how to reverse it with your own conscious efforts.'

She looked as eager as a child waiting for her bedtime story. I assured her of complete recovery and asked her to forget about surgery.

After thorough interrogation and analysis of her symptoms, especially the emotional aspect, I came to the conclusion that rather than grief or sadness of having to leave her husband, it was the feeling of being insulted for years together and breaking of her self-esteem to level zero by a narcissistic spouse that triggered her disease process. Hence, I started with a homoeopathic remedy that matched the state of her mind and body and would balance her to take on other modalities. My drug of choice was staphysagria; a remedy given for any disease arising after suppressed chagrin that has no outlet and is eventually poured out onto someone completely unrelated to it (in Vydehi's case, it was her only son), later consolidating as tumours in the body (here it being stye, fibroid, and goitre). (For more information, visit: www.materiamedica.info/en/materia-medica/james-tyler-kent/staphisagria)

I gave the medicine and asked her to return after two weeks. I also recommended a unique detoxifying, therapeutic diet (mono dieting) and asked her to join a gym where she could exercise for an hour daily. Vydehi agreed to everything like an obedient student with hope lingering in the depths of her eyes.

Two weeks later, she returned to my clinic and lo and behold, the lady I had met just fifteen days ago was nowhere to be seen. Here was a new Vydehi with a sparkle in her eyes, though feeble. There was a slight pinkish hue over her cheeks despite the pigmentation, and her gait was steady and much more energetic. Before I even got a chance to ask anything, she gushed, 'Doctor, my bleeding has reduced to seventy-five per cent and I feel energetic. I feel much better. What did you do to me, doc? Now I can go out for a job and support my son.' She talked for half an hour. I listened to all the positive changes she had in the few days.

In the end, I smiled and said, 'I did nothing but give you a homoeopathic medicine to balance your brain and stimulate your metabolism. The workout sessions and diet you have taken up have aided in mobilising your metabolism too, thereby creating a happy environment for the medicine to act. This is detoxifying your system and balancing all your organs to function optimally. You are on your highway to recovery, Vydehi, and I thank you for being such an obedient client. It is a delight to work with you. But let me tell you this, while my medicines will reverse your pathology, the ultimate healing is in your hands. Eventually, you will have to throw away your walking stick (medicine) and learn to walk by yourself.'

'I totally surrender to the process, doctor. Now I am convinced that I will get healed,' she said, her eyes glistening with unshed tears of joy and faith.

Here was another broken piece of pottery waiting to be fixed; another incredible soul who had willingly surrendered and was asking to be made whole. Now it was my role to play the potter with some pieces of gold to kintsugi this precious pot.

Given below is the outline of the awareness session that I gave her. I use this to educate all patients who come to me with any chronic disease.

The Holistic Approach to Health and Disease

The theory of the evolutionary process of health and disease on which I have built my entire career and practice may not be acceptable to the conventional norms of medicine and can even be rejected on the grounds of lack of evidence-based research. But even the most widely accepted theories are based on assumptions and for which there is very little hard evidence, like Darwin's theory of evolution. Historically, that theory probably ranks as one of the biggest assumptions ever made. It serves as the basic assumption behind all biological science and as the very foundation on which much of our accepted scientific truths rest. However, the fact that no evidence exists to prove this assumption true does not mean that the theory is invalid or not useful. I borrow this explanation from Collin C. Tipping before going into any elaborate claims on the tools I propagate. My assumptions which I have put to practical use in the last twenty-seven years have been adapted from my learning and training in medicine and homoeopathy, clinical nutrition, yoga, psychology, and the concepts of various authors and healers.

According to the WHO (World Health Organization), health is a state of complete physical, mental, and social well-being and not merely the absence of disease or infirmity. You can see that it is stated in no unambiguous terms that health is a state of feeling good at all levels and it is not enough that your physical parameters are normal. A mere discomfort in your mind or in your social circumstances where you are not fully at ease also implies that you are unhealthy or dis-eased.

As Vydehi was more concerned about cancer, I thought it was prudent to take cancer as a reference point while explaining the evolution of disease. Cancer, and for that matter, any of the so-called fatal or terminal chronic diseases do not suddenly pop up in your body and give you a life sentence of suffering and death. It takes several months or even years of evolution and ignorant neglect for a disease to finally make itself known through sensations, symptoms, and signs. To get a better idea about this, you have to understand the workings of your body and mind and how they are inseparably connected in manifesting diseases.

Awareness of the mind-body connection in diseases is by no means new. Until approximately three hundred years ago, virtually every system of medicine treated the mind and body as a whole. But later on, the Western system of medicine gained popularity which saw mind and body as two different entities. It considered the body as a machine with replaceable parts and independent of the mind. Though this viewpoint had definite benefits by acting as the foundation for advances in trauma care, surgery, pharmaceuticals, and emergency medical care, it greatly affected the scientific inquiry into the emotional and spiritual aspects of the human constitution and its innate ability to heal oneself. However, this view gradually started to change by the advent of the 20th century and researchers began to study the complex links between the body and mind. The term psychosomatic disorders came to be widely accepted but little was done in the way of finding a protocol of medicine integrating both entities. Dr Freidrick Samuel Hahnemann is probably one of the earliest propagators of the concept of the mind-body connection when it came to healing diseases. He discovered a holistic system of medicine called homoeopathy which considers the mind and body as inseparable from one another.

Before going any further, let me elaborate on the workings of our body and mind and their connectedness. As we know, our body is made of trillions and trillions of cells. Numerous cells of similar nature cluster together to form tissues, similar types of tissues get together to form organs (brain, kidney, stomach, etc.), and organs having a similar function cluster together to form systems (such as the nervous system, digestive system, respiratory system, and so on).

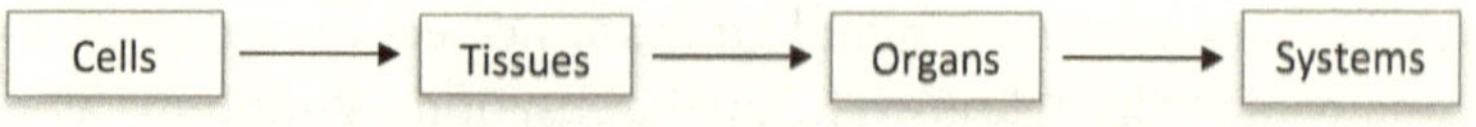

Cells, in turn, are made up of genetic material called DNA which is the fundamental unit of life. DNA pack themselves into a long chain of chromosomes and this arrangement is unique for each individual. This poses a very interesting question: From where and how does the DNA get the instructions to fall into a particular genomic sequence which differentiates one human being from the other? Try as we might with our logic, we are at a loss to pinpoint the inherent intelligence by which the DNA operates. This brings us to an entity beyond our perceptible senses, an energy that springs from an unknown zone. Einstein called this unknown zone of energy the 'field' and later physicists called it the 'quantum'. It is also called the universal energy or intelligence by metaphysicians.

In every act of creation, there occurs a transformation of energy from one form to another under the influence of this universal energy. When a baby is conceived in the womb, it is infused with an energy called life force which takes its commands from the universal energy and has the inherent capacity to coordinate itself into the different entities of the human being. This explains how a speck of DNA situated at the centre of one fertilised egg coordinates itself to multiply until a small cluster of cells is formed, large enough to begin to sort itself out into tissues and eventually into organs and systems. (Adapted from the book *Quantum healing* by Dr Deepak Chopra)

So, the ultimate reality comes down to the fact that we are animated by a form of energy called life force and its unstinted harmonious flow keeps our bodies functioning. When we die, the life force leaves the body and merges with the universal energy. Whenever there is a block in the vibration of this energy, the balance and harmony of the human body get disturbed and it shows as a loss of well-being or disease.

Master Hahnemann propounded this theory two centuries ago. He says in the 9th aphorism of *Organon of Medicine* (the Bible to a homoeopath), 'In the healthy condition of man, the spiritual vital force (autocracy), the dynamis that animates the material body (organism), rules with unbounded sway, and retains all the parts of the organism in admirable harmonious, vital operation, as regards both sensations and functions, so that our indwelling, reason-gifted mind can freely employ this living, healthy instrument for the higher purposes of our existence. When a person falls ill, it is only his spiritual, self-acting (automatic) vital force, everywhere present in his organism, that is primarily deranged by the dynamic influence upon it of a morbific agent inimical to life.' This vital force is nothing but our life force or the energy mentioned above.

So much about the body's constitution. But where is the entity called the mind situated? From our limited knowledge, we say that the mind is inside the brain but in an autopsy, you don't find a mind inside the human body. So, the mind is not synonymous with the brain, but it makes its presence known through the medium of thoughts and emotions, which are again energy vibrations. The brain is the hardware that allows us to experience them. Just as vision is for the eyes and hearing is for the ears, thoughts and emotions are the functionality of the mind. These two entities (mind and body) are very closely interrelated for the functioning of the human being.

Mind-Body Connection

Our body is composed of a broad network that consists of the brain and peripheral nervous system, endocrine system, and immune system. They share a common chemical language and communicate with each other, thereby maintaining a perfect harmony between them. Neurotransmitters like adrenalin, serotonin, GABA, glutamate, dopamine, acetylcholine, and hormones like cortisol, oestrogen, progesterone, testosterone, and the immunity boosters secreted by the lymphatic system are some of the substances secreted by different organs in our body. They transmit signals between the body and the brain to control our everyday functions from breathing, digestion, and excretion to pain sensations, movement, and emotional/intellectual activities.

Let me illustrate this brain-body connection with the example of the fight-or-flight response which was originally designed to help us react automatically in dangerous situations, such as an attack by a wild animal. When we feel that we are under attack, the body releases adrenaline and stress hormones such as cortisol. These automatically send a signal to our lungs to breathe faster and shallower, our heart to beat faster, our skin to sweat, and our muscles to tighten. Blood pressure and blood sugar levels rise automatically too and the immune system is suppressed. All these sensations propel us to either run away from the spot or fight back. This same response can be triggered in our bodies even without an immediate threat of danger. For example, when we face acute stressful situations like hearing of the death of a loved one, facing an interview or exam, or getting into an argument, the same flight-or-fight response gets initiated in our system but with lesser intensity. You may have seen people falling unconscious or just freezing in their position when they get the news of an accident or a sudden death of a loved one (flight), or they may break into violent outbursts of crying or anger (fight). The same response also gets triggered when we are subjected to chronic stress like strained relationships (between spouses, family, colleagues, or bosses), work-related issues, and long-term grief and stress (as in separation and single parenting).

On the other hand, the opposite happens when we are in a happy/peaceful environment or doing things we love like eating chocolate, exercising, having sex, or a relaxing massage. During such activities, happy hormones and neurotransmitters like endorphins, dopamine, serotonin, and oxytocin are released which relax and rejuvenate our bodies. So, we see that each mental state or emotion has a specific physiology associated with it, a positive or negative energy vibration felt in the physical body.

Now let us see how this can cause diseases or ill health in the human body. As I mentioned earlier, the harmonious flow of the vital force keeps the body functioning optimally. Any circumstance that upsets our mind or body upsets/blocks the natural flow of the vital force and causes an energy shift, an entropy. According to the concepts of natural hygiene, these blocks are called toxins while Dr Hahnemann calls it by the term 'miasm' (derived from the word miasma meaning noxious vapours or pollutant). When toxins enter inside your body, you feel lethargic or fatigued with no apparent cause. Harvey Diamond uses the term 'enervation' to describe this state. It is the first perceptible symptom that a block exists inside your constitution.

This brings us to the following questions: 'Where do these blocks/miasms/toxins come from?' and 'How do they find their ways into the human constitution?' In the answers to these questions lie the causes of all diseases under the sun. These blocks can be either inherited or acquired during the lifetime of an individual. The inherited blocks are the ones that are transmitted by parents to their offspring through genes and are present right from birth (for example, Down syndrome, Tourette syndrome, cystic fibrosis, cerebral palsy, etc.). They are irreversible, according to the concepts of modern medicine.

On the other hand, acquired blocks/toxins are imbibed from the immediate environment (epigenetics) and can come from extrinsic and intrinsic sources. The extrinsic sources of toxins include faulty lifestyle factors like inadequate nutrition, excessive ingestion of highly-processed, seasoned, or flavoured food (junk food), overindulgence in alcohol or narcotic drugs, and erratic daily routines. The other external causes include variations in climate, microorganisms (viruses and bacteria), environmental pollutants, indiscriminate use of immunosuppressive drugs, or prolonged use of hormonal and other chemical-based medicines. The intrinsic blocks come from the mental/emotional planes like childhood trauma/shock, prolonged grief, anger, fear, suppressed or repressed emotions, mental stresses of work/relations, negative thought patterns etc.

When the body is relentlessly forced to come into contact with any of these toxins, it leads to a poor supply of restorative neurotransmitters, hormones, immunity boosters, and electrolytes. Poor nutrient supply results in poor metabolism and poor elimination of waste. Then the undernourished cells die and form an accumulation of waste products due to which the body's power to self-repair gets reduced. Self-repair is done by our immune system which is essentially made up of a network of lymph nodes, white blood cells, and lymphatic channels through which flows the magical fluid, the lymphatic fluid. The immune system fights against toxins by eliminating them through unique processes of phagocytosis, autolysis, and regeneration. Our bodies constantly strive to keep us in harmony and balance through the workings of this immune mechanism. Usually, it is an involuntary process and the inherent healing capacity of the body eliminates these toxins and thereby protects us from diseases. But when the toxins that barge into the economy of our system are much stronger than the capacity of the immune system, it succumbs to them, thus creating an imbalance in the vital force and hence disease.

When the symptoms that arise from any of these causes are suppressed or left unattended, the body goes into the next stage, the stage of toxaemia, where toxins accumulate in the blood and other tissues of the body. The body and mind try to eliminate these toxins in a stage called irritation in which it activates its defensive mechanism to unload stored-up toxins. A classic sign of irritation at the physical level is the itching of the skin. Another obvious example of irritation is the inordinate urge to urinate or defecate. The skin, bowels, and bladder are clearly the most obvious means by which waste materials and toxins are removed from the body. Signs of irritation can be seen in other eliminative organs as well, for example as irregular menstrual periods or prolonged bleeding. At the mental level, signs of irritation are expressed as anger, anxiety, sadness, or mood swings.

All these warning signals are only on the functional level. All lab findings and other physical parameters would be normal during this stage, though one might feel ill. There is no damage to the organs in this phase. Unfortunately, most of us ignore such signs for years as they are not serious enough to go for treatment. However, if corrective measures are taken at this stage, to eliminate the toxins, normalcy can be restored with no treatment whatsoever. Just by making lifestyle modifications and changing your life circumstances and thought patterns will restore the balance. These changes can include modifications in diet and regimen, moving on from an abusive relationship, changing the stressful job for a better one, and forgiving and forgetting hurtful people and circumstances in life. If not, the toxins accumulate in even higher concentrations and the next stage of disease, inflammation, sets in, which is the body's most intense effort to restore itself. With inflammation, the toxins usually concentrate in a particular area of the body. The area shows signs of redness and swelling with intense pain and heat. Pain is the body's most effective warning signal to take action to get rid of faulty living habits or take steps to remove toxins from the body. Thus, we get inflammation in various parts of the body, corresponding to the body part which gets the impact of the entropy. For example, tonsillitis, hepatitis, appendicitis, nephritis, sinusitis, lymphadenitis, etc. These are indications that the body is using its reparative powers to forcibly eliminate waste products. But little do we realise that pain and heat are our most friendly messengers. Suppressing pain and heat (fever) with painkillers and anti-inflammatory drugs is the norm we are used to. Anti-inflammatory drugs don't remove pain, but only block the pathway or mechanism of expression of the vital force. When we suppress the effects of inflammations with drugs, the immune system is suppressed even more. Toxins further accumulate in the cells showing up as swellings or hardening of the tissues. This state is called induration. We call this swelling neoplasm or tumour, which is usually harmless or benign in the beginning, and the body is still in control of its cells. The body also tries to eliminate the pent-up toxins by forming outlets through the tissues and organs. This is called the stage of ulceration. Thus, we get suppurative conditions of various organs like gastric or duodenal ulcers, abscesses of glands, canker sores, skin ulcers, rectal fissures/fistula, etc. Even at this stage, complete reversal is possible by eliminating the fundamental causes that led to the state and corrective measures are adopted.

However, if the causes and destructive processes that brought matters to this stage continue, the body mechanisms start breaking down and the cells no longer remain under the control of the vital force. They leave the coordination of the vital force and intelligence of the body, and the immune system goes into a massive battle to restore the body by multiplying wildly in an unorganised manner. Unwarranted new cells are produced in a frantic attempt to rescue the body but these immature cells do not have the capacity to maintain the organism. Cells go haywire, which, in turn, alters tissues and organs in such a way that the normal functioning of the body is affected. Massive amounts of cells and tissues start getting destroyed, causing disintegration of the whole tissues in the affected part. Finally, the DNA structure of the cells gets altered and science refers to it by the term mutation and ultimately, label it as malignant or cancer. These stages have been beautifully summarised by Harvey Diamond in his book *Fit for Life* (visit. www.vpnutrition.com) as well as by Dr Hahnemann through his theory of chronic miasms. According to the theory of miasms, all diseases under the sun can be classified under its three vast ramifications, i.e., psora, syphilis, and sycosis.

Now you know how the body becomes the platform for the outer manifestations of the effects of toxins. It reacts to the inner patterns of thoughts and emotions by manifesting symptoms corresponding to the intensity and type of each of them. For example, unexpressed emotions like anger and grief literally get stuck in the throat and cause blockage and disintegration in that area (thyroid, pharynx, larynx, or neck nodes). Sexual dissatisfaction and insults manifest as diseases of the uterus, ovaries, or breasts. Fear and anxiety usually manifest in the digestive organs. This is exactly what Louise L. Hay describes in her book, *You Can Heal Your Life*, where she has a big table connecting each emotion to the corresponding body part. (For more information, visit: www.alchemyofhealing.com/causes-of-symptoms-according-to-louise-hay)

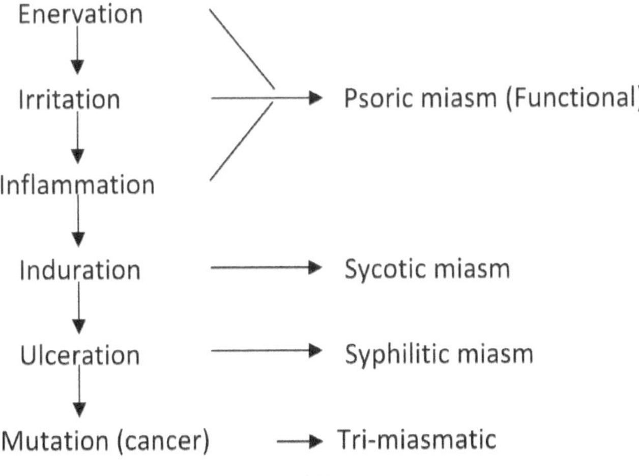

***

Coming back to Vydehi, after explaining the whole process, I analysed her entire journey. The constant stress of having to put up with a narcissistic husband together with the insults and suppression of emotions were the causes, which initiated her disease process. Depression and lack of energy (fatigue) were the functional symptoms she had at the onset. This caused an imbalance in her metabolism (enervation). The suppressed grief and lack of outlet deranged her thyroid hormones, accounting for the constant fluctuation in moods (irritation). This later led to thyroiditis (inflammation) and with the continued stress, it led to induration of the thyroid gland (goitre). If she had been able to identify the cause and remove the energy block in the thyroid, she could have recovered totally. But it was managed with hormonal tablets, a temporary external support to balance the thyroid hormones whilst ignoring the actual cause—the stress. Naturally, the imbalance had to manifest in the next most vulnerable feminine organ, which she felt was most insulted—her uterus. The sexual insults, body shaming, and infidelity from her husband affected the uterine lining. Then signs of irritation showed up as irregular periods and prolonged bleeding. This was also suppressed with hormonal drugs. Finally, the uterus started reacting by forming a swelling medically termed as fibroid (induration). This was also not addressed from the causal point of view. So, it had no choice but destruct on its own and go into a precancerous stage, as was evident from her biopsy report. If left unattended, naturally the cells would mutate and go into cancer.

Modern medicine removes the organ before it gets into that stage and that's why Vydehi's gynaecologist suggested removal of the uterus. But removing each diseased organ while ignoring the actual cause of the disease is the most monstrous way of approaching treatment in chronic diseases. It amounts to just cutting away the result of the disease while the cause still lingers. It is like closing a cracked, gushing pipe with a cork for the time being. Unless the causes that brought about her condition are not removed, the built-up pressure would again lead to leakage in some other organ of the body. Usually in women, either the ovaries or breasts are the next vulnerable organs. This vicious cycle continues until the cells start mutating. If Vydehi realised the mechanism of how she fell ill in the first place and totally revamped her mind and body, she could be reverted to total health and wellbeing.

After explaining the whole scenario step by step, I asked her, 'Does any of this resonate, Vydehi? Does it make sense?'

'Yes . . . doctor . . . yes. I now clearly understand how I got into this state. So, what is the way to reverse it? Is it possible to reverse it once and for all? I really want to recover, doctor. I want to show him that I can live and look after my child on my own. I need my son to grow up strong and unscathed from all that he has seen in this small life of his.' She was excited and prompt in her response being the intelligent lady that she was.

'Yes, dear. You just wait and see,' I assured her. The initial prodding had already begun with the homoeopathic drug and she was on her highway to healing from the outer aspect. The inner journey was to be done by her with full commitment. She had to change her mindset from being a victim to a victor and that required a real shaking-off of so many negative attributes acquired throughout life.

We took the beautiful journey of healing with the help of exercise, fasting/diet modifications, affirmations, and visualisations. And yes, within a span of six months, the cracked pot was whole again. I travelled with her for one year in her incredible journey to healing and when the normal ultrasound scan reports came for both the uterus and thyroid, together with normal blood parameters, I knew this kintsugi mom would take on life like a champion.

It has been thirteen years since our first encounter. Vydehi is now the proud mother of a well-bred young man and owner of a designer boutique, which satisfies all her material and creative desires. Once she became aware of the process of how she became sick, it was easy to guide her through the reversal process as well.

Each of the modalities will be dealt with in the coming chapters and the exercises will be consolidated in the chapter 'The Road Map to Kintsugi'.

Chapter 3

MONDAI

(The Problem Is Rarely the Real Problem)

*J*ust when I thought that I had all the inputs for my book, there came another broken pot, Simran, again a single mom warrior. I very well knew it was the law of attraction at work. The universe was responding to my intention of writing about the challenges of single moms.

Simran was going through a stagnating phase in her career as a Montessori teacher and was referred to me by a close friend. As we settled down after the formal introduction, she began narrating her problem.

'Doctor, you know that I am going through a bad phase in my profession. I have had to close down the third institution I so painstakingly developed. This has been occurring for the last fifteen years. I start ventures, reach the pinnacle of success, and then, all of a sudden, something happens and I am out of the project. I feel like a total failure. Now I am bankrupt. I don't know what to do with this life. I am also sick and really need your help, doctor.' She said and then let out a long sigh.

I had to get the whole history to reach an analysis and be of any significant assistance. So, I asked her to start from her childhood. This was her evolutionary story.

She was born into a poor North Indian family in which disparity between sexes was a common norm. The girl child was considered a second citizen and was expected to be nothing more than the *chirag* (light) of her husband's family. Therefore, Simran's brothers got the most of whatever little there was while she was blamed for everything and punished for the smallest of mistakes by her mother and brothers alike.

Her father, who was a small-scale businessman in another part of the state, one day abandoned the family forever, leaving a very bitter mother and seven little souls to fend for themselves. Simran had to put her studies on hold in order to take care of her younger siblings as their mother had to venture out to feed them. The sudden abandonment by her father and the responsibility of taking care of the younger ones imbued a rebellious fighter spirit in Simran. She desperately wished to complete her schooling so that she could find a job and become independent. Despite all protests from the community and family, she completed her matriculation at the local government evening school where education was free but that was the limit. Her mother managed to marry off the elder girls to men who were either widowers, old bachelors, or already married. This compromise was the only way to curtail the expenses incurred in the name of the double-edged sword called dowry.

Simran was considered fortunate when a rich young bachelor asked for her hand with no dowry demands whatsoever. It was like a lottery to the family but the minute Simran saw him at the bride-seeing ceremony, she knew that he was not the one for her. She begged her mother to spare her but how much could a seventeen-year-old girl with no other resource protest?

She recounted her first night at her in-laws' place. It was a big old mansion with so many rooms that one would easily get lost. The whole family, including her husband's three sisters and mother, were loving and extra cordial to her from the onset. This was very unusual in the conventional setup of that era where the new bride was mostly looked upon as an intruder and in-law rivalry reigned supreme in practically every household. The reason became evident on the first night itself.

Exhausted after the wedding formalities and a long bus ride, Simran was dying to crawl up somewhere and get some sleep. She was ushered into the bedroom by the eldest sister-in-law and was relieved to see the beautifully decorated cot. But then, Samar, her newly-wed husband, barged in with a photographer for a post-wedding shoot. It was 2:30 a.m. and this man showed no plans of calling it a day. Simran somehow managed to keep her eyes open and after all the drama, asked him the way to the washroom. The bedrooms in the old mansion had no attached ones. She got the biggest fright of her life while returning from the washroom he had shown her, which was far away in the courtyard. A dog pounced upon her from nowhere in the dark and she screamed and ran back to the bedroom trembling where she found Samar lying on one side of the bed. He was naked and masturbating so unabashedly that he didn't stop even when Simran entered. Being brought up in a very protected environment, she had never seen a fully naked man, not even in pictures. The first obnoxious sight of a male genital organ being stimulated by the man himself is something she can never remember without violent nausea and terror. She silently crept to the other side of the bed and shrunk herself into a ball all the while shivering and weeping, but the man did not flicker an eye towards her. After a while, on hearing loud, frightening snores, she turned to find him sleeping like a beast, open-mouthed with limbs flayed all over the bed. She distanced herself to the farthest end of the cot, in pure disgust and fear, and fell into a disturbed slumber only to be woken up by the youngest sister-in-law early in the morning with an all-knowing smile. Her mischievous eyes were frantically searching for bloodstains on the bed as she made double-meaning remarks that every girl after the nuptial night is subjected to. But how could Simran disclose what had conspired at night?

Suddenly, they heard the sound of crockery breaking and rushed to see what the commotion was. When Simran entered the kitchen, she saw her terrified mother-in-law standing in the corner and pleading with her son to stop shouting while a very angry Samar kept on throwing every utensil in the vicinity. The reason for his anger was that the bed tea he was served was too hot and sugarless! Simran stood there dumbfounded, not knowing what to do. Her sister-in-law slowly ushered her out of the room. She now understood why they hadn't demanded any dowry and why all of them were extra sweet to her. Samar was a psychiatric patient. The old belief went, 'Everything will be alright after marriage. Get him married and the girl will change him.' Let alone change, Simran couldn't even dare to look directly into his eyes. She thought of informing her mom about the conditions at her new place but then decided not to. At that moment what she felt was a deep resentment for her family that had literally unburdened itself with this marriage.

Simran found some solace in her very loving mother-in-law and started living as if she was her daughter rather than her son's wife. Being neglected from childhood, she revelled in the maternal care and easily merged into the family, but could never connect with Samar. Every night she would go to their bedroom, only after hearing his loud snores. But one night, she was jerked awake due to the excruciating pain of hungry, beast-like teeth cutting into her lips. She tried to scream but was hushed by being bitten even more harshly. She still cannot decipher what all transpired that night except that in the end, she was left bleeding all over the bed and bruised from head to foot, unable to even move her legs or touch the area between the thighs. The next morning, she staggered out of the bedroom in a dazed state. Her sister-in-law, who was in the corridor, saw the telltale bruises and winked at her with a teasing smile. Simran knew not how to react and just limped into the bathroom outside the courtyard, hating men and life forever.

As the days passed, the beast in Samar became more and more ferocious. He started abusing her physically even in front of his mom and sisters. However, he never approached her in bed for a long time much to her relief. He seemed content masturbating in front of her.

Simran continued living like a robot, as if all emotions had been completely squeezed out of her. Even when she wanted a change of clothes or personal paraphernalia, she never dared to ask Samar. However, her mother-in-law was very considerate and would lend her the used clothes of her daughters which infuriated Samar all the more. He would neither provide nor allow her to borrow anything. It was as if three meals a day and a bed to sleep on were more than enough for a lady to remain alive. This vegetable-like existence went on for a few more months. Samar's mother and sisters were well aware of the worsening state of affairs between them; the screams and stifled sobs behind the closed bedroom door were proof enough, but they dared not interfere for fear of being beaten up as well.

One day, Simran's younger sister came on a casual two-day visit. Samar was extra cordial and was going out of the way to please the girl. Simran smelled something fishy, as it was not at all in his nature to behave this way. Hence, she kept a vigilant watch on him and what she suspected happened on the very same night. When she ceased to hear his grunting snores in the middle of the night and turned to find out that he was not in bed, Simran stealthily scampered to the room where her sister was sleeping. There, she found Samar lying next to the little girl. The twelve-year-old was sleeping calmly, oblivious to the vicious intentions of her brother-in-law, and as luck would have it, Simran reached there just when he was about to move forward with his intention. She literally pounced on him and beat him up in front of the whole family who had rushed in. The next morning, she packed three sets of clothes and a matriculation certificate—her only possessions—in a small polythene cover and hugged her mother-in-law goodbye. The poor old woman could find no words to stop her. All she could say was, 'I am sorry, my child. Please inform him that you are leaving.' Simran didn't think it was necessary. She touched the feet of this new mother she had become so fond of and bid adieu to the house once and for all. All this while, Samar was sitting like a statue outside the verandah of the house and just kept staring as Simran walked out, hand-in-hand, with her little sister.

***

What Simran didn't know was that this wasn't the end of her tribulations. She got the biggest shock of her life when she reached home and told her family about what had happened but neither her mother nor siblings were convinced of the ghastly stories she shared. For them, Simran was making up these scenarios to escape out of a marriage she was not in favour of from the beginning. Even the incident with her sister was taken as simple brotherly affection which Simran had misconstrued. They tried to persuade her to return to Samar and even involved the local religious priests to intervene. A separated girl in the house was obviously a burden to the family and also detrimental to the future of her younger siblings, but for once, Simran was strong in her resolve and refused to return.

Fortunately, she procured a job as a caretaker in a neighbouring kindergarten which gave her a chance to venture out of the house and lick her wounds in peace. But that was also short-lived. One day, she fell unconscious in the classroom and was taken to the nearby hospital where she tested positive for pregnancy. The news came as another jolt as she didn't expect this outcome after just three nightmarish escapades of sex! She was advised by her brother to abort the child immediately as she was anyway not going back to Samar.

However, at that time, it was the mother in her that took the upper hand. She wanted to keep the baby as she felt that this way, she would have a part of her own flesh and blood in her life; someone she could call her very own and nurture.

She once again rebelled against her family and went through the nine months of pregnancy in much agony and loneliness but in the hopes of the ecstasy of holding her little one in the end. Her boy did come with a bang. It was a very complicated delivery through C-section because of which she lost a lot of blood. However, the little face of Ayaan was all she needed to propel herself into an entirely new phase of life.

Once back from the hospital, things started getting very sour between Simran and her family. Her brother asked her to leave the house, as they were not ready to take responsibility of a fatherless child. So, she rented an apartment and moved in with the baby. She could not afford to get defeated now, as there was a soul that was totally dependent on her. She resumed her job as a caretaker in the kindergarten and during work hours, she would take the baby along and leave him at the day care of the same school. This way, she could do justice to her job as well as breastfeed him during intervals.

Soon she became a favourite among the kids. The school's principal also noted her natural skill with children. One day, a little girl was punished by the class teacher and made to stand outside the classroom. The principal, who happened to be passing by, found Simran consoling the weeping kid. She was impressed by Simran's tact in tackling the little one and immediately asked her to take over as a teacher in the same class, ousting the cruel teacher who had punished the child. Since it was a private institution, quality and skill counted more than qualification. Simran was more than happy to accept the post. Meanwhile, she enrolled for a part-time course in Montessori teacher training to get officially qualified.

Life seemed to improve with the added income but the challenges on the personal level still remained overwhelming. Single moms at that time were a rare breed and the neighbours in her community left no stone unturned to defame her in every way possible. She was called an immoral lady, a curse to society, and was thrown out of her apartment. She tried to find some other place but was mercilessly rejected by every landlord in the vicinity. Finally, she managed to procure a small room at the kindergarten at the mercy of the principal.

However, life wasn't through with her yet. One afternoon, a peon rushed into her classroom to inform that her son was being taken away by a man who claimed to be his father. To her utter dismay, she found Samar at the school office, holding the boy in an iron grip. The terrified kid was screaming at the top of his voice. Simran jumped in to rescue the apple of her eye but the principal stopped her and handed a paper—a court order that gave Samar the custody of the child. Amidst her screams of protest and agony, he simply walked away with the kid.

Simran's world collapsed once again. She spent the next six months walking the corridors of every court and magistrate office to retrieve her child. Helpless and frustrated, she went like a beggar to her familial home for refuge. The loneliness was more than she could bear, but they blatantly refused and accused her of making wrong decisions in life. 'We advised you to abort the child, didn't we? Now reap the fruits of your choice,' was the insensitive remark from her own mother.

Disheartened, Simran came away but refused to give up come what may. Eventually, she met a kind criminal lawyer who took mercy on her pathetic plight and offered to fight the case free of cost. He even offered her shelter in his outhouse. After months of legal fights, she finally retrieved her boy from a slum area. When she found him, he was tied to a pillar, beaten up, mutilated, and almost half-dead. It turned out that Samar had given him off to a rural North Indian family to keep him out of Simran's reach. She still shudders at the sight of her child in that dilapidated house, in torn clothes, and with bruises all over his body. I could not even imagine the agony the mother in her would have felt at the horrifying sight.

She returned to the lawyer's outhouse with the sole intention of nursing her baby back to normal. Impressed by the relentless determination and dedication of the young mother, the kind lawyer offered her the space to begin her own day care centre for kids.

***

The undying spirit of motherhood and the need to sustain both of them gave Simran the energy to rebuild from where she had left. In a matter of months, there were more than fifteen little angels under her care. More and more kids joined in, through hearsay of the unique teaching methodology she adopted. She surely had a flair with little minds, and the children started loving her even more than their own mothers. But life could not be so easy for Simran! The next disruption came in the form of the lawyer's jealous, suspicious wife who just barged in one evening and demanded the keys to the outhouse. She suspected an illicit relationship between her husband and Simran.

On the road once more, Simran swallowed her pride and again approached her mother to allow her and her son to stay till she could find another shelter and job. Somehow, the innocent, charming face of little Ayaan melted the grandmother's resolve and they were allowed in. Though still insensitive and rude to Simran, she took an instant liking to Ayaan, much to Simran's relief.

With every crisis, miracles also happen in life to push you on. A few days later, Zayan, the father of one of Simran's students, came like an angel into her life, begging her to restart the kindergarten. His daughter was crying every morning to be taken to her favourite Simmy teacher. Many other children were giving a similar hard time to their parents. Zayan along with some other parents offered her a space to teach and she once again flagged off her new venture with renewed zest.

Zayan turned out to be a real gentleman, supporting her like nobody in her life had. He would come every day to school to drop and pick up his daughter and soon, he made his intentions clear. He openly admitted his love and admiration for Simran. Though she resisted his advances at first, she eventually became defenceless in front of his unconditional love. For the first time, she was seeing what real care and love from a man was like. Zayan was a man who simply reflected all that she longed for in a partner—compassionate, sensitive, well-read, and handsome. He also had a big backlog of struggles both at the personal and professional fronts.

'My accidental encounter with Zayan was nothing I had ever foreseen. It took me into an entirely surreal world of hope and happiness,' Simran reminisced. 'He was a patient listener and my story literally moved him to tears. For the first time in my life, I was getting a feel of real romance and irresistible physical attraction. But I could never think of an extramarital affair, being a mom myself. How could I enter into a relationship with the father of my student? How could I ruin his family? Why was this very wrong thing happening? I asked myself a thousand times during my prayers.'

She continued, 'I was older and sagacious too. It behoves any divorced person to engage in serious soul-searching before contemplating a second marriage and consider what must be done differently so that the next marriage endures. A dark cloud of insecurity, a thunderstorm of uncertainty, and a lightning bolt of curiosity become a part of you and shudder at giving this a second chance. However, the vulnerable, yearning woman in me needed the care and security this man offered. I agreed to enter into a relationship only if he would legally marry me to which he readily agreed. Being a Muslim, it was not at all a problem to get married as per the Muslim marriage act but we decided to initially keep it a secret from his first wife and Ayaan.'

She went on to narrate about the next phase of life. 'I stepped into the relationship with shaky legs, carrying the comparison baggage of my first marriage like an inexorable shadow. Then began a quest on how to pick up the broken pieces and see what could be made out of them. There was a profound desire in me to sustain this new partnership.' She paused, took a breath, and continued, 'Life began anew with Zayan visiting my house only during daytime or on holidays, trying to build a relation with Ayaan and showering him with love and presents. Slowly my body started transforming. I started taking care of my beauty and health after years, going out for walks, and attending to my diet. Now I wanted to live, to love, and be loved like never before and was determined to fill all my wounds with the ethereal energy of Zayan's love. The physical transformation within months was a miracle in itself and I realised that there are men like Zayan too on this earth.'

She looked away, teary-eyed, unable to continue. I deciphered the rest of the story in between her sobs. Simran's mother played her sinister role once again by feeding negative stories to Ayaan about Simran, making him gradually hate his mother. However, Zayan was firm and determined to make this relationship work. He did his best to coax her mom and everyone in the family. But alas, there was also this other person in his life, his first wife, who eventually got the news and hell broke loose. It was then an unending fight between the two wives, as well as between Simran and her son. Every time Zayan came over, his first wife would know of it, being informed by none other than Simran's mother. The lady would create big scenes, making life impossible for all, which was only natural. On this side, Ayaan and her mom would not have food for two to three days after Zayan's visit which made Simran feel that she was the greatest sinner of the millennium. Ayaan started drifting away and denied her access to even his room. The only person she lived for now considered her his worst enemy. He hated his mom for marrying Zayan.

Life was becoming impossible. She needed both of them but ultimately, the mother in her won. She couldn't afford to lose Ayaan. Therefore, she decided to divorce Zayan for the peace of mind of all concerned—his wife, her son, and their families. A heartbroken Zayan tried to dissuade her in every way and even offered to divorce his first wife but Simran would not hear of such an injustice. She took it all unto herself in the hope that Ayaan would forgive her but the damage his grandmother had done to his vulnerable mind was irreparable.

***

Now, Simran was left with no one to lean upon; no family, no son, and no partner. The school she had started also dissolved on its own. Falling into an abyss of depression and anxiety, she lay for days together in utter confusion and helplessness. Though under one roof, Ayaan never came anywhere near her and even called her a total failure. He started visiting his father Samar on his own and Simran realised that she was losing her only hope and support in life. Yet the mother in her could only love and forgive him. He was in his formative years and she knew the havoc those changing hormones could cause to an already disturbed mind. His education was extremely important and so the warrior mother once again ventured out, this time starting her own school with a loan from the local bank. She also joined the same bank as a part-time insurance agent. Finally, she didn't have to be at the mercy of anybody and her innate teaching skills attracted kids from all around. The enterprise expanded in one year to an academy with fifteen staff members and state-of-the-art infrastructure. The resources she needed came in the form of donations from parents and organisations. She became a small celebrity in her community and an epitome of inspiration to all single women entrepreneurs.

The following year, she decided to further her skills as a Montessori teacher and handed over the administration to the young manager of the school to go abroad for three months. Ayaan was anyway not communicating with her and his grandmother was taking good care of him. She had subtly trained him to be on his own from childhood and hence did not feel guilty about leaving him for three months. After all, it was for him that she was running the school and toiling day and night as an insurance agent.

A very triumphant and confident Simran returned to pick up from where she left off, only to find that the young manager had taken over the institution. The staff was also somehow coaxed into believing that Simran was detrimental to their aspirations. The school was running on voluntary donations till then, as Simran believed that it was not right to forcefully collect fees from parents. She felt that by running an academy for kids, she was answering to her calling in life and therefore money was not a factor; and it did come in sufficient amounts in the form of donations. But the manager had changed the whole machinery in the three months. He had started collecting huge amounts of fees from the parents and the staff members were immensely happy at the sudden rise in income. She sensed the startling change in the attitude of the staff from that of unconditional love and commitment to consumerism, profit-mindedness, and mechanical conduct of duties. The extremely loving and cordial atmosphere where children had the freedom to scamper to the teachers for each and every one of their needs was gone. Simran just looked around, wrote a letter to transfer the power of attorney to the manager, and walked off.

***

It was at this point in her life that destiny decided to make us meet. When Simran came to me, she was an emotional and physical wreck, bordering on the brink of insanity. Her miseries were further augmented by her constant battle with rheumatoid arthritis and a big ovarian cyst. As her voice trailed off after the long monologue, the pent-up tears started flowing incessantly. She struggled to control herself and I could see that one tissue box wouldn't be enough.

After allowing the uninterrupted catharsis, as usual, I started my job. 'Tell me Simran, what do you feel now?' I asked.

'I feel totally stagnated. I have lost interest in doing what I enjoyed most, to be with my students. Now even seeing children sends a shudder up my spine. I don't feel any soft emotion for anybody. I am always fighting with my mom. I know that she has done a lot for me and my son, but why does she have to judge and criticise everything I do? If she had co-operated, at least I could have lived a beautiful life with Zayan. Then there is my son. Didn't I dedicate my whole life to him and sacrifice everything for him? Now he hates me and finds his father better. He sees me as a total failure in life and even insults me in front of his friends.' She continued, 'The manager boy, how could he cheat me and snatch the school, my brainchild? I feel totally defeated, doctor. Everything I undertake ends in failure, after the initial promising impression. Either I have to abandon it or it is taken away from me. I don't have the grit to fight with life anymore. I feel stuck, exhausted, numb, and totally indifferent to everyone and everything, especially those whom I love the most—my son, my mom, and my students.'

Her words were just like reading the description of the drug sepia in the *Homoeopathic Materia Medica* (textbook of the pharmacological symptoms of medicines). I still cannot fathom how Master Hahnemann and his contemporaries could so scrupulously record even such subtle symptoms of the mind two centuries ago! In the symptomatology of sepia, it is vividly depicted how a woman who is subjected to constant stress and sexual suppressions finally becomes blank to emotions, indifferent to the most loved people in her life, always angry and resentful. Physically, she is a telltale picture of gynaecological complaints, develops butterfly patches across the cheeks with a very rigid blank facial expression, and exhibits all the symptoms associated with hormonal imbalances: menstrual irregularities, fibroids, cysts, and tumours in the breast, uterus, ovaries, etc. (For more information, www.materiamedica.info/en/materia-medica/james-tyler-kent/sepia)

I needed no further interrogation as a homoeopath to decide upon her medicine. Simran was sepia personified and I knew a single dose of it in high potency would magically click her out of her stagnated mental status. It would act on her reproductive system and shrink the ovarian cyst. It would also balance her immune system, curing her rheumatoid arthritis (which is an autoimmune disorder).

However, the drug would only help her out of the disease and depression. Her dismal life circumstances would remain the same unless and until she was made aware of the subtle but very negative patterns of life she was subjected to till now. There was a connecting thread of defeat, abandonment, and grief running throughout her life. A dismal pattern of constant failure and being cheated and put down was present throughout her history. Obviously, she was coming from a space of lack and low self-worth.

I could see the vicious cycle of events in her life and where the healing had to begin. Years of experience has taught me that at the core of every broken person, there is a basic underlying pattern or problem which can be elicited from his/her inner-child analysis. Once this problem is identified, the kintsugi work becomes transparent and doable, with little effort. The next one hour was spent educating Simran and suggesting the optimum solutions for her next phase of life. The following is the summary of what I discussed with her and the points I highlight to every client with similar needs.

'The problem is rarely the real problem,' said Louise L. Hay.

Everyone has problems. The world seems to present you with a vast number of problems, each requiring a different answer. These problems seem to be on so many levels and coming in such varying forms and with such varied content that they seem totally unrelated to each other. However, on introspection, it is seen that the problems in your life are nothing but projections of your past experiences. Your only problem, no matter what form it takes, lies in your perception of the experiences in your past, your core memories even from intrauterine life, which your conscious mind is not even aware of. Only by perceiving the underlying constancy in all your problems will you understand the means to solve them. So, the initial step towards finding a solution to all your problems is to go into yourself and make a thorough analysis of your past, starting from the moment of your conception.

As we know, our mind is composed of a conscious part and a subconscious part. When an infant is born, only the subconscious mind operates and the reasoning or conscious part of the mind is inactive. In fact, the subconscious mind gets activated the moment we are conceived in the womb of our mother. It imbibes everything that is fed to it without a filter, like a computer's hard disk, and stores them in neatly piled up folders to be accessed later on. This subconscious part, which is about ninety per cent of our mind, is what rules a child up to six years of age. It does not know how to reason or reject unwanted matter. So, every childhood experience gets absorbed into it till the age of six. The conscious reasoning part of the brain which logically thinks and filters unwanted data becomes active only after six years.

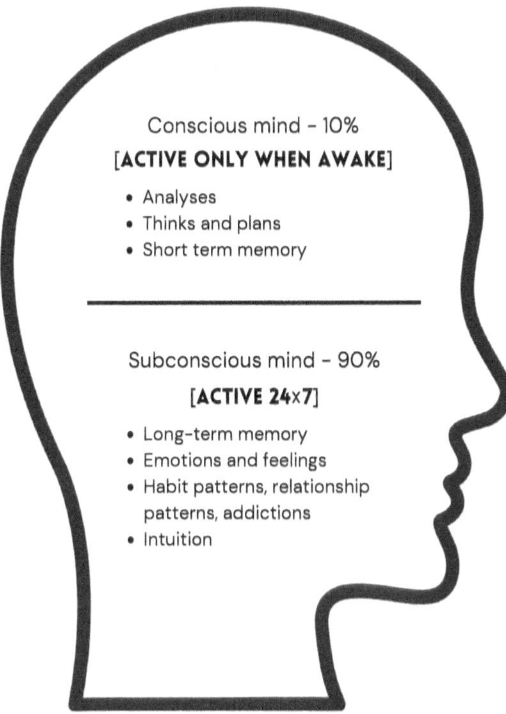

During intrauterine life, the sounds around us, our mother's stress levels, the abundance or deficit of the 'feel-good' hormones and neuropeptides, our nourishment or the lack of it, infections, etc. influence us. Immediately after birth, it is our parents, immediate family, and caretakers who play the most important roles in shaping our mindsets. As we grow out of infancy and into childhood, we absorb a great deal from our extended families, caregivers, friends, pre-school and early school mentors, and religious institutions. And though we may not have conscious memory of all that happened in our childhood, there is an inner child in each of us, holding on to every good or bad instance that we have gone through. Our later experiences in life will reinforce these beliefs and form our own 'script' for how our life should be. We carry these immature scripts and decisions with us into adulthood and they dominate our lives. Eventually, we tend to attract and replay similar situations in our lives when we grow up.

'Let me explain with a few examples. As children, when something goes wrong and we are blamed/punished for it, we tend to believe that there is something wrong with us. With time, this idea turns into the belief that "I am not good enough". We carry this false belief with us into adulthood and start demeaning ourselves. This leads to several issues including low self-esteem, poor body image, mood swings, emotional imbalances, problems with boundaries being too rigid or too weak, problems with eating, self-destructive habits, psycho-sexual difficulties, identity problems, rebellious attitude, being a perennial victim, intimacy and commitment problems, and a general lack of trust in oneself and others.

'Again, if a child is brought up by a father who always says that money comes the hard way and you must work hard for it and then also very little comes your way, the child grows up with this belief and always has a block towards attracting money or being rich. If he grows up in a family where everybody body-shamed him for his looks, he grows up to be an adult who loathes himself and does not have any self-esteem. If he is ridiculed and scolded for his academic underachievement at school compared to other kids, he starts hating himself and this carries on to his adulthood. Eventually, he becomes an underachiever everywhere and in everything he undertakes. This happens in every area of his life, from relationships to career as well as health.'

So, you see, ultimately, it is your belief systems and subconscious thought patterns that make you what you are. You have around 80,000 thoughts per day of which 80 per cent are repetitive and depend on the attitude you were brought up with. If you were in a negative environment throughout your childhood, 80 per cent of the repetitive thoughts are negative and these thoughts create your reality. And this is the root of all problems we face in later life.

I concluded and turned to Simran. She looked worried. 'Is there no way to come out of our childhood scripts, doc?' she asked anxiously.

'Yes, dear,' I assured her. 'The good news is that we have the capability to erase these scripts, revamp our thought processes, and install an entirely new mindset with our conscious efforts. By simply understanding our childhood scripts/patterns and then inserting new thought patterns in the form of words that are positive, we can create a new story for our life. Such positive words and statements that help you overcome negative thoughts are called affirmations.' (We will be discussing this in detail in a later chapter)

Simran was eager to know more about affirmations and the solutions to her seemingly unending problems. So, I attempted to give a detailed analysis from my point of view. Traversing through Simran's life, it was evident that the pattern of constant failure, abandonment, and victimhood started from her own home. The root of all her problems were the subconscious beliefs from her childhood conditioning like, 'I am not good', 'I don't deserve to have a good relation', 'I don't deserve to have money', and 'I am not loved'.

The inherent notion she grew up with was that the girl child doesn't deserve the best of anything in life. As she said at the beginning of the story, she was always blamed and scolded by her mom and siblings for no fault of hers. She was always made to feel that she was wrong and not good enough. This was compounded by her father's abandonment. Due to this, insecurity and the fear of abandonment were so etched in her subconscious mind that wherever she went, she was either ousted or she would have to ultimately leave, be it her first husband or her second, or all the institutions she started. She never felt that she deserved abundance as poverty was a part and parcel of her childhood. There was a negative, ingrained belief about money that ruled her subconscious mind due to which she attracted the same or similar circumstances in life. For example, she was reluctant to take fees from the parents of her students, which led to the financial crisis each time.

I continued to clarify further, 'So, you see that the actual root of all your problems starts at the subconscious level, and to tackle all the existing problems in your life, you have got to go to your past, analyse, and undo them. You need to learn to let go of all past conditioning and outgrow the need for acceptance and validation from others.

'No matter how old you are, you have a little girl within you who is very tender and needs love and acceptance. No matter how painful your early childhood was, loving the inner child now will help you heal. In the privacy of your own mind, you can make new choices and think new thoughts. Thoughts of forgiveness and love for the inner child within you will open new pathways, and the universe will support you in your efforts. It is not an easy process but not impossible either,' I concluded.

By then, Simran was convinced of the evolution of all the problems in her life. I could now introduce her to the other tools of self-love that included inner child meditation, the negative messages exercise, mirror work, and forgiveness exercise. It was not at all easy working on a lady who is a self-made leader and coming with so much grief, resentment, and depression. Yet, she surrendered to my sincere efforts and reported a great sense of well-being and positivity within a short time. She ultimately healed herself from the inside out with her own diligence and efforts.

Simran has now migrated to another country as a highly paid Montessori teacher. She is cured of her physical ailments. Sepia had done its job. Her buttons do get pushed at times, but she has all the strategic tools to revert to normalcy in a jiffy. Samar passed away after a harrowing liver disorder and Ayaan now realises his mother's love and sacrifices for him. He is a smart boy, pursuing his studies in a hostel. Simran still aspires to have a true soulmate in life and does her affirmations religiously. She also has a beautiful relationship with her mother, after understanding where she came from. As an abused, abandoned wife and a single mother, her mother could only react to life as she did. Simran was able to completely forgive and embrace her with so much compassion and love. She was also able to forgive Samar who was essentially a hapless psychiatric patient. He probably inherited the disorder from his schizophrenic father who had committed suicide when Samar was still a child.

Finally, Simran is a healed soul, totally in sync with her life's purpose, and wafting on a cloud of love and peace. She updates me occasionally over the phone or social media and I know there is no more stopping this ball of fire.

Chapter 4

YURUSHI

(Forgiveness - A Gift to Yourself)

I was working on my bulky, post-delivery body at the local gym in a desperate attempt to revive my old, vivacious self. Julie, my enthusiastic and high-spirited trainer was pushing me beyond my comfort levels to help me achieve my goal of sixty kilograms from a whopping eighty kilograms. During one of those sessions, in came a bundle of bubbling energy, whom I will call Gauri, lighting up the whole room with her infectious laughter and non-stop lively chatter. She was remarkably plump with a curly boyish crop, fully confident, and comfortable in her own skin. There was no way this woman could be ignored even in a crowded room. Her pop of curly hair and the disproportionate size of her limbs and chest were enough proof to an experienced physician to conclude that she was a cancer survivor who had undergone chemotherapy and surgery.

When Julie introduced us, I greeted her with a polite, 'Hi, Gauri.'

She responded with an energetic, 'Hello, doc. Nice meeting you.' Her next statement was as startling and unabashed as she was. 'Well, I am a divorcee and single mom of two. I live nearby,' she said breezily and then added, 'I left that cheating bastard of a husband for good, doc.' She continued running on the treadmill and giggling simultaneously as if she had cracked a big joke. The nonchalant mention of her ex-husband and the fact that he was now living with a much younger girl was really amusing and out of the box.

I pretended not to be surprised and said, 'So what? Forget it, dear. By the way, what's the secret of your positive energy and sparkling eyes Gauri? You simply fascinate me.'

It was now her turn to be amused. She replied, 'Your response comes as a surprise to me, doc. I typically get curious looks and sympathetic glances wherever I go. Snoopy strangers often quiz me about my family, husband, children, and other irksome personal details. So, I have developed this habit of blurting out my story right away to everyone so that I can evade those awkward, intruding queries.'

Gauri and I bonded over our workout session and established an invisible yet strong thread of mutual respect and understanding. She talked about how she lost one of her breasts to cancer, her struggle with weight, and how she was working towards fitting into medium-size clothes again. I learnt that she was a victim of domestic violence for years at the hands of her husband, who also separated her children from her. Her strength emanated from fighting for her rights at the end of which she was a highly successful businesswoman and propagator of women's rights. I also got to know that she was a foster mother of a teenage girl and ran a very successful software consultancy firm with twenty supporting staff members. To top it all, she had been awarded the best women entrepreneur of the year by an international organisation. She truly was living proof of an empowered and enlightened woman who had discerned her purpose and passion in life. I immediately realised that she would be an ideal subject for my book but did not mention it then.

Shortly after this encounter, I became her physician for a severe attack of dengue fever from which she recovered within days with the homoeopathic remedy, rhus toxicodendron. From then on, she became an ardent believer and supporter of homoeopathy. The foundation for a lasting relationship both at the professional and personal levels was established. So, after a while, when I asked for an interview, she readily complied.

Here is Gauri's survival story.

***

Gauri was married off to the son of her father's business partner, who was a successful surgeon in the UK, much against her wishes. Being an ace student with a gold medal in engineering, Gauri had what it took to fend for herself. Yet, she had to give up on her ambitions to appease her father.

'Though I was not at all prepared for a marital life, I knew I wouldn't be able to escape the inevitable event in my typical traditional upper-class family setup,' she said. Her marital existence was a half-minded plunge into oblivion and a far cry from her spiritual inclination and disinterest in men.

After an ostentatious wedding ceremony that involved an exchange of expensive gifts including a BMW car, a flat, cash, and gold, she shifted to the UK. 'The reality of life struck when I was confined to the four walls of the house with a baby boy in my lap and my very efficient surgeon husband was always on duty at his hospital,' she said. Her dream of pursuing a career was squashed as she soon gave birth to their second son and became inundated with the responsibilities of being a mother and homemaker.

She continued, 'Saurav wanted nothing but sex and money from me. He demanded money on various pretexts like for buying a car, setting up a hospital, or starting a new business venture. I was supposed to arrange it through my father each time, and if I refused, I was brutally abused and beaten up in front of the kids. Moreover, my father wouldn't hear anything bad about his son-in-law. Instead, he blamed me for being headstrong. The gentleman image Saurav had created among my family members was so convincing that nobody would believe anything I say. Away from familiar surroundings and with no one to confide in, I had no other choice but to stay put in the same atmosphere,' her voice choked.

When the kids got older, she gathered enough courage to venture out and find a part-time job in a software company. Saurav protested initially, but with her excellent academic records and calibre, he could not gaslight her for long. The brief stints of freedom at the office were a huge relief. She made a few friends and started living a new life, albeit without any support or encouragement from her husband.

When her colleagues quizzed her about the marks on her body from the abuse, she would dismiss them as accidents. 'I could never disclose that I was being brutally raped by my own husband every night and that too multiple times. Life was becoming an insurmountable hell with his other torture tactics. Yet I put up with it all to protect my children from the legal procedures of a police complaint.'

The continuous stress, however, took its toll on her health. One day, she noticed a lump on her breast and showed it to Saurav, who, after an act of concern so false that Gauri flinched, arranged to get it investigated. Her worst fears came true with the inevitable cancer diagnosis and advice for immediate removal of the breast. Unwilling to take responsibility for her treatment in the UK, Saurav sent her and the kids to India. After the harrowing flight back with the younger boy clinging to her bosom throughout the journey, her dad took over all the treatment expenses including chemotherapy and surgery, but she terribly missed and craved the company of a loving partner to help her tide over the nightmarish ordeal.

She recounted, 'Only when I emerged after all treatments with a bald head, one-sided flat chest, and an arm twice the size of the other due to some complication in the lymphatic drainage, Saurav made his appearance from the UK. He had quit his job there and planned to rejoin his previous hospital in India. As soon as he landed, he made me sign a bunch of papers that he claimed were for my health insurance. Little did I know that they were life insurance policy papers, with him as the nominee. It was a devious plot to usurp the money after my death. He knew the prognosis of my case and that the doctors had given me only six to ten months to live, which nobody told me at that time.'

Gauri's woes only increased when Saurav came to stay with the family. She was not spared of sex even in that weak state. Her condition worsened and she got weaker in the coming months. Another test revealed a metastatic lesion in a lymph node that required yet another round of surgery and chemotherapy. By the time she could come to terms with her condition, Saurav had started an affair with a junior physician who was almost half his age. Even then, he kept on demanding more money on the pretext of her treatment. That was when Gauri decided to divorce him. She realised that if this kept going on, her children would be left with nothing. She informed her father about her decision to separate but it was not well-received, as expected. The family did not believe that a husband who 'stood by her' through her illness could be so inhuman. However, she finally convinced her father to intervene and that was when Saurav showed his true colours.

'After the prolonged court procedure, he squeezed out more money and property from my father before agreeing to sign the divorce papers. By the end of it all, my father succumbed to a massive cardiac arrest, leaving me a complete orphan,' she said, looking away to hide the tears. After a brief pause, she continued. I was very sick, financially broken, and helpless. Saurav won the custody battle for the children, citing my illness and financial status as reasons. Thus, I was left all alone in my father's flat; the only property that was in my name.

'That night was the worst night of my life, doctor, and the best one too. I wept for hours together on the pillow and then staggered to the altar where I keep my favourite Krishna statue. I asked him with all my heart to take me away from this world, never to see any more suffering, and then passed out at the altar.' Her voice cracked as she spoke.

From that abysmal pit, her world was completely transformed by a cell phone message that woke her up at the crack of dawn. It was an ad promo whose heading read: 'I am the TRUTH. In fact, I am the only truth.' Gauri saw it as divine intervention . . . as if God was speaking to her through those words and it made her feel secure and supported by some invisible force. This motivated her to forget her pains, leave behind her past, and look forward to life ahead.

'The next day was an altogether new world for me. I decided that I would forget about my illness and never think of death again. I first got a stack of books to pursue my passion for reading that I had missed all those years. I called my children and was relieved to know that they were safe in boarding school, away from their evil father and his new partner. Hence, I could meet them whenever I wanted. From that moment, I haven't turned back, doctor,' she said triumphantly.

One of the guiding forces on her new journey was the guru, whom she discovered from the book, *The Autobiography of a Yogi*. She began to eat well and do yoga and meditation. In a short while, she managed to open a small consultancy firm in a rented building. Gradually, her business picked up and to the astonishment of doctors, Gauri became completely cancer-free. But for Saurav, these developments came as a great shock as they foiled all his plans. He threatened to kill her if she did not give him the only property she had—her flat—to recover the amount he had paid for her life insurance policy. When he did attempt to take her life by subtly removing her car brakes, she managed to sabotage his malicious plan. From then on, she stood strong against him and did not succumb to any of his threats.

'Saurav still cohabits with that young physician and harasses me, but now I am beyond his reach. I have support from everywhere, including the police and women's rights organisations here,' Gauri said proudly. I am free to meet my children and I take them home whenever I want. Those are the moments I cherish above all in my life. By the grace of God, both my boys are unscathed and balanced in life which is the only thing I have ever wanted for them. I am a proud mom, doctor,' she said and then reached for the handkerchief to wipe away the tears of joy that had welled up.

The next instant, her expression changed to one of bitter hatred and she asked, 'But my one question remains unanswered, doc: Why doesn't he ever let me live in peace even after the separation and usurping of all my assets?'

To answer that question, I had to give a short awareness session, after analysing her life script. I observed that Gauri was very bitter and filled with so much hatred and resentment for her ex-husband. She needed to learn the tool of forgiveness to really move on. She had to forgive him, the circumstances, and other people who caused her unending suffering in order to gain the true peace and harmony that she was working towards. Though she had bounced back from a deadly disease, emerged stronger, learnt to love herself, and be assertive, she still had not forgiven her ex-husband. Only if she let go of her inner resentment and anger towards him would she get closure. Unless and until she releases/let go of that person from her consciousness, the same pattern will go on replaying in different forms. He would go on with his tactics and she would have to endure it till the end. She had to embrace that one ultimate tool of forgiveness to really move on in life and put an end to his harassment.

I proceeded to establish my point and started by asking her about how she embraced spirituality at such a young age. She said that the disharmony in her parents' matrimony was the trigger. Her mother was a victim of in-law rivalry and her father was a workaholic who was never emotionally available. Her mother suffered from severe bouts of depression and had gone through several years of psychiatric treatment before finally succumbing to cancer. She would spend hours in the puja (prayer) room in the house and found solace venturing out to the nearby temple every day along with Gauri. After her untimely demise, Gauri was raised by her dominating and vicious paternal grandmother. Her dismal childhood made her averse to marriage and men and hence, she never fell in love with anyone. She religiously followed the ritual of going to the temple every day even after her mother's demise and found immense peace and tranquillity in the serene corridors of the temple.

'Can you see a connection?' I asked her. 'Your cancer, your divorce, and your spirituality?'

She looked puzzled and replied, 'No, doc. I don't understand.'

'Okay. I am going to share my view of what I have deduced from your narration till now. Are you ready for some self-analysis?' I asked with some apprehension.

'I am all ears doc,' she said and leaned forward in the chair.

Encouraged by her keenness, I began to break down her life into parts. Being brought up in a dysfunctional family, Gauri was inculcated with images of two women personalities, her mother and her grandmother, both completely in contrast to one another. While her mother was a quiet victim, her grandmother was the strong and manipulative one. Gauri started identifying people based on only these two personalities and that influenced her response to her own life situations. She played the helpless victim in the first phase and gained the strength to survive in the second phase of her life. Her cancer was a result of not just genetics but also the constant state of stress, resentment, and sexual dissatisfaction, leading to DNA changes and mutation of cells (epigenetic factors).

Gauri was at a loss. 'But what does all these have to do with the harassment I am still facing at his hands, doc?' Her doubt was only natural.

That's because you have not yet released him and your past from your consciousness Gauri. You need to forgive him and let him go. This is the only way you can begin life with a fresh, clean slate without any baggage from the time gone by,' I reiterated.

Gauri still remained defensive. She could not understand how she could forgive someone whom she hated so much. And after contemplating for a while, she asked, 'How will I handle the torture Saurav is still subjecting me to? After snatching almost all my properties and trying to murder me, how can I think of forgiving him?' Her question was again totally justified.

'Yes, it is difficult, Gauri. You hate him and cannot, even for one moment, think otherwise. It is totally understandable, but by holding on to your resentment and hatred, you are not helping anyone. It just destroys your peace of mind and withers you into bits and pieces. At the end of the day, you are harming only yourself, while he is carrying on beautifully with his life.'

I continued, 'Try to see life from Saurav's side. He was an innocent, sinless baby when he came into the world. His childhood experiences and influences are the factors that made him what he is today. Nobody is born a womaniser or abuser. We don't know what his subconscious inputs were, the circumstances in which he grew up, and other factors that shaped his character. Try to see him as an innocent boy who got moulded into what he is today by his negative influences. Feel compassion for that little boy, forgive him and let him go. Now that you have already thrown him out of your life, you need to let him out of your consciousness as well. Think of him as a stepping stone to reach the place where you are now. All the trials and tribulations laid by him has made you the heroine you are today, a source of inspiration to scores of helpless women. You did not become the best entrepreneur of the year by sheer luck. It is the grit and resilience you acquired from all that you had to face in your life that made you what are.' I paused to look at her. She nodded in agreement.

Now that she was a little more receptive, I went on to explain the benefits of forgiveness. 'By forgiving him, you will emerge stronger, more peaceful, and grounded. Forgiveness allows us to liberate ourselves from the chains of hurt, bitterness, and resentment. It helps us become peaceful, embrace our past, and integrate ourselves into the future with a positive outlook. Forgiveness is a healer because it replaces negative emotions with positivity which, in turn, translates to physical, mental, emotional, relational, and spiritual healing and well-being.

'Once you embrace forgiveness and do the simple exercises I suggest, you will see a shift in life, Gauri. Saurav will automatically vanish from your life,' I assured her.

She still seemed sceptical but agreed to follow my advice and act accordingly. I realised that to convince an intelligent and educated, woman like her, I would have to impart the value of forgiveness in self-transformation with scientific proof. I went on to substantiate my point by recommending a YouTube video by Vishen Lakhiani, the founder of Mindvalley foundation, which is a transformational coaching centre. The video showcases the story of an employee who looted money from his firm and how he was pushed to declare bankruptcy. Vishen literally cursed the employee and was holding so much hatred that he was not ready to forgive this man, come what may.

Incidentally, he came across a group of scientists conducting an experiment to access the brain waves of people to help them reach the alpha state of consciousness, similar to what monks and competent meditators achieve over many years. In this experiment, the individual is put into a chamber, hooked up to a machine, and then given autosuggestions or hypnosis. During one such session, they found a rapid transformation in the brain of a lady who suddenly seemed to exhibit a positive, alpha state. When they quizzed her about her thoughts, she replied that she was forgiving her mean ex-husband because of which she progressed to a level of peace and calmness so rapidly, much to the amazement of the scientists.

Vishen found it intriguing and tried it himself. After spending five days in the chamber, he testified that he forgave everyone including his parents, children, colleagues, and his own younger self as well. After this, he was able to attain new heights of peace and abundance within a year and completely transform his life. He was able to forgive the employee who had stolen from the firm simply by thinking from that person's perspective. Maybe he needed the money badly or he may be coming from a space of lack or poverty and was forced to steal in his childhood. Through this reasoning, Vishen felt compassion for him and his resentment and anger gave way to forgiveness. From then on, he has been practising the tool of forgiveness every single morning and accessing the fruits of it in every area of life. This is popularly known as the *kensho* technique. (Video link: www.youtu.be/a7fIaCA3Qr4)

Gauri seemed fascinated when I finished the narration. So, further substantiation of my theory became easy. I went on to talk about Worthington, a clinical psychologist who identified the outcome of forgiveness on the peripheral and central nervous systems using several scientific techniques. I also suggested a few books like *Forgive and Forget: Healing the Hurts We Don't Deserve* by Lewis Smedes and the works of authors like McCullough, Elizabeth Conway-Williams, and Jon R. Webb, all of whom talk about different aspects of forgiveness.

By this time, I had managed to capture Gauri's full attention and enthusiasm. Now that I knew that she was more receptive to the concept of forgiveness, I could introduce the concept of radical forgiveness which is different from traditional forgiveness. When we use the term forgiveness in the traditional way, we imply that one person is the forgiver while the other person is a sinner. Here, the victim feels that the sinner has wronged him in some way and condemns him for it and forgiveness is a benevolent act which the victim bestows on the victimiser. But this form of forgiveness does not liberate the victim completely.

What really works is radical forgiveness, a concept that came into my life through a book called *Radical Forgiveness: Making Room for the Miracle* by Collin C. Tipping. Radical forgiveness takes the position that nothing went wrong and as a result, there is nothing to forgive. In traditional forgiveness, it appears as if something bad has happened and there is a need to condemn that goes along with the willingness to forgive, whereas in radical forgiveness, there is the willingness to forgive without the need to condemn as there is no victim-consciousness.

Let me explain. Hurt and bitterness arise in relationships when one person is victimised by the other. It can be a partner, in-laws, parents, friends, or even your own children. We may feel totally victimised in the relationship and blame the other person for our miserable life. But the real culprit turns out to be our childhood experiences and the theories made up by our subconscious minds. We tend to attract people who are compatible with our childhood trauma/subconscious beliefs. We replicate them in later life in a never-ending array of relationship problems.

To totally extricate ourselves from this vicious cycle, we need to hit rock bottom and then rise like the phoenix bird from the ashes of suffering and victim consciousness. Then we understand why certain people and circumstances are/were in our life. We realise that the other person—the victimiser—was needed to project our misinterpretations on for us to learn and grow.

The worst situations that prevent us from being happy often contribute to our healing, and the most troublesome people in our life end up as our teachers. In the process, we get to learn about ourselves and heal. This realisation leads to a change in our perception and then we stop being the victim. Then there is actually nothing to forgive and we release that person/circumstance from our life once and for all. In fact, we learn to thank the people and circumstances which imparted the lessons we invariably needed to complete our sojourn on earth.

For instance, in Gauri's case, she attracted a partner who was the same archetype as her father and she replicated her mother's role, that of a victim, in this equation. She had a lot of negativity built up from childhood due to living around an insensitive father and a mother who was suffering from depression and cancer. These childhood experiences led to her hatred for men and marriage. Her inclination towards spirituality was, in fact, an escape mechanism to evade men. What she attracted later in life were just projections of her negative belief patterns. She needed to be totally victimised by Saurav and hit rock bottom before she could realise and own the immense strength she had inside her all along. She had to experience the whole process and learn to let go of her internal victimhood before she could feel completely liberated and healed. What appeared to be cruel and nasty behaviour from her spouse's part was exactly what she needed and had indeed called forth. Saurav was inevitable to bring out the true potential Gauri was capable of.

I finished off and took a moment to observe Gauri's reaction. There was that contented smile of realisation and acknowledgement of my exposition on her face. I sighed with relief as my efforts had finally borne fruit.

Gauri wholeheartedly accepted my suggestions and surrendered to the process of travelling back to her childhood through guided meditation to radically forgive her husband, mother-in-law, grandmother, father, and most importantly, herself. She embraced every event and person, including her husband, and thanked them for the lessons they taught her. This was all that she required to free herself from the shackles of the past. I was glad that I could be of some help on her journey towards a fulfilling life and promised to send her a copy of my manuscript once it was ready. (These exercises are explained in detail in a later chapter, under the headings 'Inner Child Meditation' and 'Forgiveness Exercise')

***

The two hours I spent with Gauri seemed like a lifetime. Here was a true ambassador of courage and resilience and a role model for women suffering domestic abuse. Her journey towards self-healing and her rebound from life's disappointments was apt material for a complete self-help book. As we hugged goodbye, I was unable to hold back my tears and inwardly saluted this kintsugi mom.

I conclude this chapter with a line from the book, *A Course in Miracles*:

'Forgiveness is my function as the light of the world. I would fulfil my function that I may feel happy.'

Chapter 5

JIBUN O AISURU

(Love Yourself in Order to Heal Yourself)

Though I have met hundreds of women with their own unique survival stories and helped many of them to move on to the next phase of their lives, it never intrigues me any less when I hear a new one. The varied and immense potential of every woman is still a mystery to muse in awe, over and over again.

As I finished writing Gauri's story on my laptop, the doorbell rang and in came Maria, one of my comrades turned client. I had invited her over for an interview as I had decided that her life story would be the next chapter in this book. She had also requested a consultation for her chronic migraine and other ailments. We had been associating for different social activities and I knew that she was a single mother who has been through heart-rending struggles. I also knew that she was a successful content writer. But that was all I knew. From a physician's perspective, I needed to know her inner journey.

Maria was looking over my new collection of succulent interior plants—a recent passion—and all the lovely blooms outside the window. 'Beautiful place, Haseena,' she mused in admiration.

We were in my dream home-cum-office, an abode I had created for myself. Long years of wandering and nomad-like

93

lifestyle had lost its charm and I had finally settled into my small cosy home. Maria was all compliments for the simple decorations I had painstakingly done in the small space—the feng shui items and my altar that comprised of nothing which would stamp me into a particular religion. I was simply proud of the abode I had created for myself and wouldn't exchange it for a palace.

'Well Maria, how about the interview? Are you ready?' I asked.

She said nothing, just smiled, and then opened her large handbag and pulled out a paper file that seemed like a manuscript. She handed it over to me and said, 'Haseena, I pondered over your request and tried to stack up my life story episode by episode, but I thought it would be too vast for you to pen down. I remember you saying that you are specifically writing about the survival strategies of single moms. So, I thought jotting down the most relevant parts of my life would make the whole process easier for you. It was a total catharsis for me in itself. Do read it, Hasee, and if you still want more information, I am as ready as ever for your interview.'

Phew! That was great as my job was half-done. I rummaged through the neatly written pages and admired her calligraphic skills. 'That is so fantastic of you, Maria. I forgot that you are a writer yourself and that too a proven one.' I thanked her profusely for the thoughtful effort.

'All the very best, Hasee. I will be eagerly waiting for your published work. Let me take your leave now. My children are waiting.'

'Children?' I asked in surprise. 'I thought that you have only one daughter, Natasha?'

'Oh!' she giggled amusedly. 'I meant my children at the special education school where I volunteer for storytelling and sewing classes. I have two hours of class today.'

I admired this lady from the bottom of my heart for the way she managed to escape unscathed after so many traumas in her life! I eagerly waited for a prolonged free time to go through Maria's narrative, as I didn't want any interruptions in between.

Here is Maria's story in her own words.

***

I was married off to a successful businessman from a reputed family at the tender age of seventeen, a time when I was just out of my teddies and barbies and wafting in the fantasy world of romance and Hindi movies. As any obedient cultured Indian girl of that era, I had neither the insight nor the audacity to have a say in the prospect of marriage. I willingly, in fact, a bit enthusiastically jumped into it and started the life of an ever-pleasing good wife and daughter-in-law. Since it was a joint family much like mine, I found no difficulty merging with the culture and routines of my new home. Kenz was a good and caring husband but was always busy, being in charge of the family business and hence was practically unavailable. I could go about the days as I did in my own home, but I knew nothing about marital life. I didn't know how to love a man as a lover or wife should. Everything was routine and mechanical and before I knew it, I was pregnant and the following nine months went by in a jiffy.

Natasha was born and she was a bundle of joy for the family. I did relish motherhood and the joys and gratifications that go with being a new mother, but I was simply flowing with the tide of life, as every well-bred girl does. Kenz was totally entangled with business problems, and I started feeling neglected and worthless. Life was drifting like a boat with no oar, no goals, and no aspirations. I was just going through the mundane daily chores, looking after Natasha, and catering to the needs of my in-laws with nothing to get excited or happy about. Until one day, the inevitable happened.

Kenz had gone out on a business trip outside the district and did not return even after the expected time. Though I wasn't emotionally attached to him, a strange knot was building up in my stomach and there was an uneasy restlessness, which increased with each passing hour. There were no cell phones at that time and no provision to know his whereabouts. Suddenly the landline rang and I rushed to it for no apparent reason, just an impulsive, intuitive act. The person on the other end unceremoniously broke the news without even enquiring to whom he was speaking. Perhaps it was a police officer or some other official, who asked, 'Is this Mr Kenz's house? I called to inform you that Mr Kenz has met with an accident. He is no more. I am sorry. Please come to the location.'

I froze and stood there screwed to the floor with the handset dangling down the table. My father-in-law grabbed the phone and I could hear shouts of panic and shock from all sides. The house turned into a shackle of grief in a fraction of a minute but I felt benumbed and was unable to even cry. My life had turned upside-down in the blink of an eye.

After the initial shock and mourning period, I started feeling that I was no longer a part of my in-laws' family. I became more and more uncomfortable with each passing day and felt like a burden to them. I was uneducated. I had no skills and was completely dependent—financially and emotionally. It was at that point that I regretted my decision of stopping my studies to get married. I felt like an outcast in the family, though nobody explicitly verbalised it. However, I overheard a few visiting elder ladies commenting that I was a bad omen for the family and Kenz's untimely death was due to my ill luck. It was a heart-wrenching moment of total insult and a thunder-like blow to my self-worth. Yet, all I could do was cry silently and grieve.

Everyone thought that I was too young and deserved another life partner, including the naïve me. It was all part of the machinery of the orthodox culture I was brought up in, which believed that 'a woman needs to have the address of a man to be self-worthy'. So, empty-handed, I came back to live in my ancestral home with Natasha, so that my parents could look out for my next groom.

Time was now hanging heavily with nothing to do except wail in self-pity and anxiety about the future. I pondered over taking up a job to keep myself engaged, but with just my matriculation qualification, job prospects were practically nil. Thanks to some influential relatives, I eventually managed to secure a job as a primary school supervisor in a distant hill station boarding school where Natasha could also be accommodated. That was a break and solace of some sort. The job was not strenuous and with my natural skills with children, I started enjoying life to a small extent. Two-year-old Natasha became Nutty for all students and staff members there and she grew up with so many mothers and friends. Later, she got enrolled as a student with a fee subsidy and I was fortunate enough to save a little for the future.

Three years passed uneventfully but once again, the monotony and closed lifestyle seemed overbearing and the meaninglessness of life started creeping in. Back home, my parents and family were frantically on the lookout for another groom and I was all the more willing to give another chance to matrimony. Many proposals were considered but I was fascinated by Sam, a handsome and charismatic widower with a mentally-challenged son. My instinct of having a way with children and that too with differently-abled ones coaxed me to believe that this was my mission in life. Sam also seemed like an ideal partner for me. I went into marriage the second time filled with hope and great expectations.

I assumed and wished that this second chance at matrimony would be the dream life I imagined. I had to leave

Natasha at the boarding school because Sam felt that Natasha and his son would not get along. With all the pains of having to leave her, I nonetheless found solace in the fact that she was safe with her foster mothers and I plunged into my new life with gusto.

Karen, my new seven-year-old son, was a darling. He needed help from changing diapers to feeding but I easily fitted into the role of his mother. We had shifted to another part of the country post marriage. So, nobody in the neighbourhood even guessed that he was my stepson. That was the rapport we had between us.

The fact of the matter is that you get married to find happiness for yourself, but somewhere you want to make the other person happy as well and with it, your happiness takes a back seat. I loved and admired Sam. His happiness meant the world to me. I would do anything for him and that included taking the best care of his child.

Sam, as I had imagined, was charismatic but a bit too much! He was too popular among the lady circles and slowly, the playboy side of his character started unravelling with each passing day along with his other vices, viz. alcoholism and drugs. I was taken for granted as Karen's caretaker and nothing more. He quickly climbed the ladder of success at his work front, now that he didn't have to spare a single minute for his son.

One night, Sam shifted Karen to our bedroom, the reason for which I couldn't decipher at that time but later realised that it was his tactic to avoid me in bed. He was slowly drifting away. Now from being the angel who had manifested to take care of him and his son (in his own words), I was relegated to the position of an unpaid servant and nanny.

Karen soon entered his teenage phase. Due to the play of hormones, which the helpless kid knew not how to control, he started exhibiting sexually advanced behaviour which I found hard to handle. He had also physically grown a lot.

I begged Sam to hire a male caretaker to help me out with Karen, but all my pleas fell on deaf ears.

One day, my father came visiting unannounced and saw my plight where I was virtually reduced to being a maid. He broke down in front of me, but at the moment, what I felt was a silent grudge. Couldn't he have investigated thoroughly about Sam's character before bringing in the proposal? Couldn't he have analysed that when Sam refused to accept Natasha as his daughter, there was an insensitive side to him? After all, I was too young and naïve to probe and analyse things. I guess he realised his mistake as he sat there, totally helpless.

***

As months passed, Karen's behaviour became more and more troublesome. He started sexually attacking me at the most unexpected moments like while I am having a siesta or working in the kitchen. I lived in constant fear even though I loved the child and knew that he was helpless. During this time, Sam's friend, Harsh, who was a frequent visitor to our house, became my confidante and I started sharing things with him. Our friendship blossomed and for the first time in life, I was getting to know the care and security of a strong man. After one long night of verbal and physical assaults by Sam, I decided to leave him and informed Harsh. He helped me abscond from the place and even accompanied me to my hometown. The twelve-hour journey brought us even closer.

My parents were naturally shocked but since papa was aware of my situation there, he didn't persuade me to go back. I was back to square one with no job, no money, and again single. However, by the grace of God, Natasha had become a strong and intelligent girl, and I was spared the guilt of having to leave my child in the boarding school. I resumed my meagre work at the school just to escape the intruding eyes of society and support myself. Harsh remained a good friend but as our relationship progressed, I sensed a change in his attitude. He wanted me as a mere presence, with no identity, while also keeping his wife and son. I was not at all willing for such a life to just satisfy my biological needs. I demanded that he accept me legally if at all he was interested in continuing our relationship. But he was too bothered about his social image, even though his marriage was a disaster. Eventually, he did divorce his wife and I thought we could finally be man and wife, but he wanted a girl from his own religion and started having a relationship with a lady in his office. I was heartbroken for the third time.

I used to wait for hours just to see his messages pop up on the cell phone screen. I would wait, unashamed, even when I knew that he had just slept with that woman. I was so desperate and vulnerable and therefore clung to this man as if without him, I would collapse. But Harsh was very comfortable playing with both me and the new woman in his life and was not willing to change his ways. I could no longer take the stress and fell into depression. To my family and outer world, I fell into depression because of my separation from Sam, whereas it was Harsh's infidelity that was affecting me. They took me to a psychiatrist who prescribed a whole bunch of medicines and even gave a fancy name for my disease, which I don't even remember now. The psychologist convinced me that I needed all those medicines to become 'normal', the yardstick of which is still a mystery to me.

During those sleepless nights, I used to watch Christian prayer channels and request them through the phone to pray for me to bring back the love of my life. I used to go to tombs of Muslim saints (which I realised later had nothing to do with true Islam belief) and to Hindu temples of all deities, where they squeezed out money from me to conduct their rituals of tantra and mantra to reclaim my man (which again had nothing to do with real Hinduism). In my desperate longing for love, I was becoming a victim to any and every atrocious superstition.

It was during that period of total confusion and uncertainty that an astrologer's site and phone number popped on my phone, promising solutions to every problem in life. Being already vulnerable, I leapt at the opportunity and dialled the provided number. The so-called astrologer picked up the phone at the other end and gave me the details of the site. He asked for my birth date, time, and place of birth, which I eagerly shared. This man, who seemed like sixty-five to seventy years of age, analysed my *kundli* (horoscope) and said all the customary jargon, which, at the time, didn't make any sense to me. That talk extended to one and a half hours and I poured my whole life history to a total stranger, a person whom I had never seen and knew nothing about.

After the initial jargon, he just pierced into every mask and wall I was hiding behind and uncovered every nook and corner of my life like a counsellor would, from my widowhood and divorce to the next dysfunctional relationship with Harsh, my tryst with depression, and the woes of bringing up my helpless child amidst all the chaos.

The first thing he asked me to do was to collect all the psychiatric medicines I was having at the time and throw them into the dustbin there and then. I was doubtful and hesitant, as I knew not what my moods would do to me without medicines. But he very confidently convinced and coaxed me into shoving them into the dustbin, if at all the conversation was to continue. I didn't want to lose this man of knowledge and readily complied.

What he said after that seemed like rain on a hot summer noon. He said, 'Madam, it is because of your strength and courage that you are still alive and working. If it were someone else, she would have taken her own life or ended up in a mental asylum. You are just reacting to your life situations just as any sane woman would. You have gone through so much in life. Throw away those pills and thank God that you are still alive and healthy.' These words were like music to my ears. I felt like he was the only person who understood me. It was like a messenger sent by some divine interplay. This relationship is still continuing in my life. This astrologer has become my counsellor, philosopher, friend, and godfather.

I know that this entire interlude had nothing to do with astrology or predictions; it was just a hub where I could pour out all my vulnerabilities with no fear of judgement, have an empathetic ear to listen to, and receive kind words of encouragement and solace. I haven't met this man in person yet. I still consider his voice as the voice of the divine, which appeared at the right time to lift me up from the abyss I had fallen into.

Later, I read the book *Eat, Pray, Love* by Elizabeth Gilbert and found a striking similarity in our stories where she meets a fortune teller in Bali who forecasts her future and everything happens as predicted, and she finds her soulmate. I started wishing for the same miracle to happen in my life but no such thing happened. No lover came to lift me up to the seventh heaven. Also, Harsh left me but I still harboured dreams of him coming back. Once again, the astrologer angel came to my rescue and patiently convinced me to move on. After all, I had a daughter to look after. By then, Natasha was a little lady and I feared that my bitter experiences would affect her outlook on life, which it did in the end. She grew up to be a girl who detested men and the idea of marriage. She was totally into academics and nothing else. She procured a scholarship to go abroad for graduation and just slipped away from my life.

I am alone now. I still wish to find true love. As of now, I have a very good friend, Mark, who is a fifty-five-year-old lonely widower. I am taking up small assignments like content writing and voluntary work at the special education school to get through my days.

***

This was the abrupt end of her manuscript. The information in it was insufficient for me to get at the crux of her case to prescribe the accurate homoeopathic medicine for her migraine. I needed finer details. So, we met again a few days later.

'That was just a story for the reader, but I need a glimpse of your inner journey, Maria,' I observed, getting straight to the point. She looked confused.

I continued, 'Don't worry, dear. Now I am speaking as a homoeopath. I need to embark upon the homoeopathic drug which will cover your migraine and other ailments. Together with that, we will go forward with the self-healing modules which are appropriate for you. Now tell me, what was your mental status and physical reaction to all that went on in your life till now? You can take your own time. Don't answer in a hurry.'

She contemplated for a long while before answering. 'Well, Haseena, after the death of Kenz, there was a deep sense of insecurity and a longing for love. That's why when I met Sam, it seemed like an ideal situation. I could also relate to his mentally challenged child. I thought I would enjoy giving love to that poor boy and in return, be loved and respected by Sam for the seemingly difficult sacrifice I would be making. But it turned out that Sam needed only an unpaid nanny for his son and a bank from where he could always withdraw money in the name of dowry. I felt so deprived, humiliated, and insecure once again, yet I could not share it with anyone in my family as it was my second marriage. Also, my papa would have been devastated by my failure at this second chance.

'With time, Sam's open seduction of other women and constant insults progressed and I became depressed and started weeping all the time. Then started this nasty headache, which would go on for days and it was only much later I realised that it was a migraine. I then started getting fatigue bouts, dizziness, and mood swings which was diagnosed as advanced hyperthyroidism. In the ten years I lived with him, I had to undergo a complete thyroidectomy and hysterectomy. I am on lifelong medication to maintain my thyroid hormones. Now, I have developed a breast lump and this irritable bowel, which is so disturbing. I can't enjoy any sort of food.'

The evolution of her medical history was clear. The suppressed emotions had accumulated in her most feminine organ, the uterus, as well as the metabolism maintaining organ, her thyroid. The arterial congestions due to stress led to migraine headaches. Each of the outcomes of prolonged stress and emotional suppressions were either removed or palliated with medicines. So naturally, her breast went into induration and the digestive system became incapable of assimilating so much stress, resulting in irritable bowels.

I could see the dismal pattern of the evolution of her relationships as well. Somewhere along the line, she had lost touch with herself and forgotten to love herself. She was searching for love everywhere in vain and falling into dysfunctional relationships in her search for it. She enjoyed nurturing and giving love and that's why she was being pulled into relationships where she could play the role of a nurturer or mother. Little did she realise that it was she who required a lot of nurturing and mothering. All the while she was trying to find validation by giving it to other people. It was crystal clear that disappointment in relationships and abandonment were her subconscious patterns.

'Maria, will you believe me if I say that you come from a space of lack and deprivation of love? Do you realise that you are endlessly chasing that elusive love and each time, you end up losing the very thing you crave? Let's see the script of your subconscious mind from your childhood and see where this sense of lack came from,' I said.

She was not able to assimilate my theory and hence I took her through the inner child meditation and analysis.

Here is her very dysfunctional childhood script. She was born into a rich, aristocratic family as the youngest of four children. Her parents had a smooth marriage, mostly due to the efficiency of her mother who was an ever-pleasing, spiritual lady. Her father, though a very genuine person, was only a passive presence who failed to impart the much needed strong paternal and emotional support. She had an elder schizophrenic sister who flipped between episodes of horrible violence and utter depression. The whole family revolved around this child and her treatment, leaving Maria in the shadow of loneliness and a sense of neglect. She would crawl up in a corner of the room during her sister's violent outbursts after being mercilessly thrashed by her. But even then, their mother had no choice but to pacify the diseased one. Maria remembered how she used to weep throughout the night alone in her room, writhing in physical pain after the beatings. Many times, she would approach her mom for some cuddling but she was always busy catering to the older child. Poor little Maria would return to her cold bed, feeling unwanted and abandoned.

I asked a few more questions to get clarity about the homoeopathic drug that would cover all her mental and physical symptoms. Natrum muriatricum—the drug given in cases of long-lasting grief, unrequited love, and disappointment in love—was my first choice for Maria (For more information, visit: https://www.materiamedica.info/en/materia-medica/james-tyler-kent/natrum-muriaticum). I asked her to return after two weeks and observe the changes.

***

Maria religiously took the medicine and reported reduced intensity of headache and better energy levels in her follow-up visit. She looked bright and fresh sitting opposite me in a pink shirt that accentuated her beauty even in middle age. Now she was ready to take up the next healing tool. I opened my drawer and pulled out the heart-shaped mirror I always keep handy. I gave it to her and asked her to look at the reflection for a little while and tell me what she felt.

'I don't feel anything. I am just seeing my face,' she said.

'Okay. Look into that mirror once again and tell yourself, "I love myself exactly as I am." Just forget that I am sitting here,' I said.

She looked on for a while and then replied, 'But I don't like myself, Haseena. I want to put on a little more weight. I want to get rid of these pimples all over my cheeks. I hate myself for not being able to be a good mother to Natasha. I hate myself for being in relation with Harsh out of wedlock. I hate myself, Haseena. How can I love myself?'

'What else do you need to feel good about yourself?' I prodded further.

'I want to get rid of these headaches. I want to relish the food I eat without the fear of having to run to the toilet each time. I want to get rid of the hot flushes. I want to get rid of the mood swings I still have, despite having my astrologer to lean upon. I need to have a better earning job. All my work gets stuck due to this nasty headache. Hence, I don't have the confidence to take up any major content writing work consistently because I am not sure that I can complete the work in the stipulated time frame. I crave a partner who loves me unconditionally. Marriage is not my cup of tea anymore but I crave for a truly loving relationship. I also need Natasha to realise that I have always loved her and want her to find a really good partner.'

That was a long list! 'So, you can feel love only if you have all these?' I asked her. 'Okay. Then take the mirror once again and say to yourself, "I am willing to change. I trust the process of life and I am safe." Say it aloud three times.'

She conceded like a little child and I went on to explain what I had in mind. 'Maria, you have been led to think that you are not lovable. You see, you never thought that you deserve true love and always feared losing it, which you did ultimately, every single time.

'Every experience, every relationship is the mirror of a mental pattern that we have inside us. Your childhood where you felt unloved and fearful because of your sister's mental disorder has triggered this pattern in you: the fear of loneliness, insecurity, and the craving for real love and never getting enough of it. So, the initial step on your healing journey is to learn to love yourself. The more you know how to love yourself and trust life, the more life will love you, support you, and guide you.

'The majority of people frantically search for love everywhere, except within themselves where it is always hidden. You are very powerful. You have the power within you to help create the kind of world you want. It is the realisation of one's worth and self-love that paves the way for every enlightening human experience on earth.'

I continued, 'Maria, first of all, you need to discard the dark veil of fear from your system once and for all and replace it with love. Love is the opposite of fear. The more we are willing to love and trust who we are, the more we attract those qualities. When we are on a streak of really being frightened or upset or worried or not liking ourselves, everything goes haywire in our lives. The same phenomenon plays out when we love ourselves unconditionally. Everything starts to happen as we desire. We get up in the morning and the day flows beautifully.

We need to love ourselves to really take care of ourselves. We have to do everything we can to strengthen our hearts, our bodies, and our minds. We must turn to the power within us. As we learn to love ourselves and trust our higher power, we become co-creators of our lives along with the infinite spirit of a loving world. Our love for ourselves moves us from being victims to being winners. Our love for ourselves attracts wonderful experiences to us. Things come to us easily and effortlessly. Self-love culminates in the all-encompassing, omnipresent feeling of universal love. This is the essence of every scripture ever written on earth, the message of every messiah and metaphysical teacher, the root of all religions and sects. If only every Siddhartha (seeker) could become a Buddha (the enlightened one), the world would be basking in an unending spirit of peace and bliss.' I finished off with my philosophical monologue to find Maria looking earnestly into my eyes.

'So, what do I do about it, Hasee?' she asked. It was evident that she was eager to know more.

'Are you ready to change your mindset, Maria?' I countered.

'Sure, dear. Who wouldn't want to end this life-long yearning for love and acceptance?' she said with hope.

'The mirror you are holding in your hand now is the first tool that will take you to that inner journey of self-love,' I said and then invited her to one of my workshops based on the philosophy of Louise L. Hay. I went on to explain the twenty-one days of mirror-work which is a beautiful tool to change the very wiring of our subconscious minds.

After her initiation into self-love through mirror work, she was amazed to see profound changes happening in and around her. Now she was ready for deeper work and so I led her through other healing modalities that included affirmations, visualisations, inner child meditation, and the Ho'oponopono technique.

Four months later, Maria reported with a handful of achievements she thought would never happen in this lifetime. One of them was the miraculous change in her relation with her schizophrenic sister. She visited Maria out of the blue with a bowl of biryani that she had specially made for her. She even stayed for one week and never picked a fight.

It was the first time in the last twenty-five years that they had been together for so long. She also willingly got admitted to a mental health centre, much to the relief of the whole family. All of them were wonderstruck at the unexpected turn of events.

On the work front, Maria collaborated with a special education institution and is working there as an instructor. She is learning sign language online to fulfil her aspiration of teaching deaf and dumb children. She is also getting a regular flow of freelance content writing work both from within the country and abroad. To top it all, she has never had an attack of migraine after the medicine. And the best part, Natasha is now married to a wonderful guy and has settled in the Netherlands. Maria is all set to visit the happy couple once the Covid-19 travel restrictions are lifted.

***

I thank the universe for making me a stepping-stone on Maria's journey to self-love and total healing, which has made her a lightworker for the benefit of differently-abled children. She has finally found her purpose in life and now knows why Kenz, Sam, Karen, Harsh, and Mark were sent to her.

If Kenz was alive, she would be a dissatisfied, passive homemaker in a big joint family and would have died a very ordinary death. She needed Karen to teach her what caring for differently-abled children looked like. No institution could have given her that first-hand experience of taking care of such a child, not from her own womb, round the clock. Sam taught her to come out of the victim-consciousness and set boundaries. Her relationships with Harsh and Mark had to end because both of them were actually living off the love and nurture Maria was providing them. They were victims themselves and not capable of imparting true love. Each and every one of them were inevitable to teach her the much-needed lessons to uncover her ultimate calling and true purpose.

Now that she has learnt to love herself and do only what she loves, she is so much at peace. She has established a real connection with divinity, which propels her to do everything with conviction and love. She has understood that she is not made for marriage and cherishes her freedom more than anything. So, now she revels in her single status and has dedicated her life to differently-abled children. She says that the moments spent with those children are the most meaningful and enjoyable parts of her life. She loves travelling all around the world with like-minded women and has already covered half the planet. She is full of gratitude for all that has happened in her life. Her earlier question to the universe, 'Why me?', has been replaced with 'Why not me?' That's how much empowered she feels now and is ever-ready to take up any and every challenge that comes along.

Chronicles and testimonials of such conviction and clarity are the greatest returns on my journey as a healer and I sing with seamless ecstasy and abandonment the song of gratitude by Karen Ducker. (YouTube link: https://youtu.be/lf9vRwf2254)

'Thank you for this day, spirit. Thank you for this day. Thank you for this healing, this healing, this healing day.'

Chapter 6

WABI-SABI

(In Imperfection Lies Perfection)

Reetha came into my life as my accountability partner while I was learning the intricacies of book writing at an online writer's workshop. In the initial conversation over the phone, the impression I got was that of a very anxious and over-enthusiastic fashion designer who wanted to market her products through her book. It struck me as a surprise when she told me that she was a single mom of three grown-up girls. Here was another synergistic association in which I got one more kintsugi mom story to put before all of you.

Reetha turned out to be an extremely successful entrepreneur with a turnover of forty crore rupees per annum. The anxious undertone in her voice was due to her confusion about the topic she had selected to write a book on. I slapped myself for once again jumping to conclusions on first impressions; a bad habit I am yet to process even after so many years in the healing profession, where unprejudiced observation is a must.

***

Reetha's life story was nothing short of a fairy tale. Born and brought up in a very secure, close-knit family on the outskirts of a beautiful and culturally rich province of North India, Reetha had it all—beauty, brains, money, and security. Doted and cared for by parents and siblings alike, her childhood and teenage years were picture perfect. At twenty-one, she got married to Rohan, a handsome, smart businessman, and shifted to a southern metropolitan city. Rohan turned out to be the dream husband a woman could wish for and her cup of happiness was full to the brim.

Soon, three talented beauties were added to the family. Reetha was a super homemaker and would complete her household chores in a jiffy, which left her with ample time for herself. She used this time creatively to acquire new skills—in addition to graduating in Kathak dancing—with full moral support from Rohan. In no time, she became a reputed fashion designer in the city. Rohan, who was in the construction business, encouraged her to try out interior designing for his architectural ventures as well. In due course, she was initiated into many more unexplored areas of life and everywhere, she proved her mettle and established herself as an undeniable presence in her family and social circles. But never in her wildest dreams did she imagine the 360-degree turn her life would soon take.

***

The devastating catastrophe took place on an exhilarating family trip to Bhutan where death, the uninvited visitor, arrived in the form of a cardiac arrest and took Rohan away at the prime age of thirty-nine. Reetha, as any other widow would do, stood aghast and lost for a short while but realised very soon that the strength of motherhood can cast out every setback in life. At the time, her youngest daughter was just two years old and the eldest was nine. She had to wiggle out of her cocoon of grief and self-pity for their sake and boldly took over Rohan's construction company but, in a matter of few days, she had to face a grim reality. The company was going through a downward spiral and was on the brink of bankruptcy but Reetha was firm in her resolve to give the best to her daughters. She didn't want them to feel deprived of the luxuries they were used to with Rohan around. So, she virtually came out of her comfort zone and pushed herself far beyond her limits. Actually, it was also a neat escapism from the grief and vacuum left by Rohan's demise.

However, a few months into it, Reetha knew that depression was taking over. She could neither perform well nor could she get accustomed to the authoritarian approach of the other partners in the company. This professional dynamic was new to her as she was so used to being the queen of her house. I remember her telling me, 'Whatever position a husband holds in his office, be it the CEO or president, at home, he is at the feet of his wife. He is all "Madam, darling, and at your service" before his spouse.' When she said this, I could imagine the self-respect and dignity Reetha enjoyed in her life with Rohan and why she could not bow down to any authoritarian figure.

Though her parents had shifted to her place and she had all external support, she was breaking down internally. Her life support had been taken away forever and to handle the emotions and multiple needs of three girls single-handedly was not an easy task, especially with the then global scenario of recession and total revamping in the financial sector.

Reetha plummeted into a dismal abyss of depression and self-imposed seclusion. She lost interest in life and in taking care of herself. Subsequently, her boutique became unpopular as the delivery of products was getting delayed, leading to dissatisfied customers. She didn't even notice this setback while whining away in her own cocoon of isolation. She would sit for hours together in the puja room fighting with God, asking him the reason for putting her into so much misery.

Days turned into months, but the constant grief and stress refused to leave Reetha and it started affecting her physical health as well. To top it all, she fell down a steep flight of stairs, injuring her spine beyond repair. She was bedridden for six months and was advised surgery, but Reetha was simply not willing to go in for it. Even while writhing in pain, she refused to go through the procedure as the doctors could not guarantee a total recovery. She intuitively knew that there was a way out and one day, while idly switching through channels on TV, she happened to hit upon a seminar by a famous metaphysical teacher and yoga master. She listened to his discourse with full attention and immediately called the number scrolling down the screen and enrolled for the yoga class and meditation sessions. That became a life-changing experience for her. It was the first golden fixture between the broken pieces of china.

She is still a living miracle for the surgeons who had sentenced her to a lifetime of handicapped existence if she didn't undergo surgery. Not only that but she also became an ace performer in the yoga academy and eventually got trained to become a yoga instructor herself. There, she happened to meet a Reiki master under whose guidance, she learnt the art of distance healing and got a certification in it as well. With the renewed boost of confidence and health, she revamped her boutique and harnessed the best weavers of Tanjavur to create a brand of bridal designer wear, which soon became the talk of the town. She also started an entirely new construction business as the sole shareholder and in no time, the company assets skyrocketed from the brink of bankruptcy to a multi-crore empire of which she now reigns as the undisputed queen.

It was as if life was unfolding like a beautiful flower before her, one petal at a time, taking her through trajectories she had never envisaged. Her three girls had also grown up by then and two of them were helping in her business. One was handling construction and the other daughter was handling the boutique. The youngest one was in her last year of graduation.

However, there were more challenges awaiting Reetha on her journey ahead. When demonetisation was declared by the Government of India in 2016, it collapsed the entire economy of the country and cast its inexorable shadows on every enterprise, including Reetha's. Unable to meet the salary demands of employees and other expenses, she had to sell many of her assets to keep going. She was also in the process of arranging and planning the wedding of her eldest daughter. As the wedding date neared, she became restless. Being a reputable name in the industry meant that no compromise could be made when it came to the pomp and show of the marriage. All the prominent personalities in the construction and fashion industry had been invited and this panicked Reetha even more, but as usual, she surrendered everything to the higher power that always nurtured and guided her.

The wedding happened on the prefixed date and everyone who attended the function commented that it was something out of this world. There was a sense of heavenly serenity and beauty at the occasion. The cost-effective, simple yet elegant ceremony, without compromising on any of the fun and frolic, was exemplary. Reetha received praise from every guest and was also asked to take up event management for some of their children's marriages.

She sat in meditation that night and thanked God for all the guidance and unexpected turn of events that had made the wedding a grand success. She slept blissfully after months, talking to Rohan, as she always did, at the end of the day. To her, Rohan was still by her side, guiding and encouraging her at every step from the other world.

***

Much time passed after the event, but the discussions about the fantastic ceremony did not subside in her social circles.

Everybody wanted to know how this single mother managed it so flawlessly and systematically. That's when she decided to consolidate all her knowledge and skills in the form of a book. To be an author was a long-cherished dream and she joined the writer's workshop where I was also a member. When the session on the topic selection for the book came, the academy suggested her to write on her business skills and ways to promote her business as a wedding planner because that was the input she had given to the mentor. However, on thorough introspection, she found that she could not resonate with the topic. She had already completed three chapters about event management but as the days went by, she was getting stuck.

It was at this juncture that we became accountability partners and happened to connect. Over the conversation, she expressed her confusion and asked earnestly about the progress of my book. I told her that I was writing on the topic of healing, which resonated with my life purpose and that too for a specific group I totally identified with—single mothers with health issues. That was her light-bulb moment. There was a sudden silence over the other end of the phone and I thought the call got disconnected. But Reetha was very much on the line. Then, with a voice grave and thoughtful, she spoke, 'Haseena, so do you feel that I should rethink the topic I have selected for writing? Actually, I am a born motivator and my yoga sessions and talks attract people to me though I have not trained myself to be a life coach of any sort.'

'Think over it, Reetha,' I said. 'You are the one to decide that. However, I would suggest that you write what you are truly passionate about and can connect with at an emotional level so that it beautifully reaches across to the reader.' We spoke for nearly two and a half hours that evening and called it a day at exactly 1:11 a.m. We both mused over the time, which was an angel number, indicating that our interlude was divinely guided after all. Reetha came to the realisation that business was her livelihood whereas healing was her passion and if at all she had to fulfil her purpose of being an author, it would have to come from her heart and her heart was always tuned towards healing and social service.

My role in Reetha's life was limited to those couple of hours. I was just a mirror to look into and help her find her true calling. Our friendship continues, and we do occasionally connect over the phone.

Over the next few months, I saw that Reetha had started her own online hub with a mission to help people find peace, harmony, and healing within themselves. She calls herself a 'situational life coach' and is currently involved with several podcasts, live chat shows, and online yoga sessions. She is all over social media and is rising in popularity with each passing day.

***

After writing this incredible story of survival and resilience, I sent it to her for approval. She was only happy to be a part of my chain of kintsugi moms and thanked me profusely for being a signpost at a crucial junction in her life. Her teaching memoir hit the market successfully and has helped many hapless women navigate through the challenges of life with courage and hope.

As a coda to this chapter, I wanted her final take on life. 'What do you think of your life till now, Reetha?' I asked.

Without a single moment's hesitation, she replied, 'I see that all the things that happened in my life had a purpose beyond my understanding. In imperfection lies all the perfection. If I hadn't gone through all the challenges in life-the loss of my beloved, my depression, my spinal injury, financial crises, and ultimately the demise of my mother who stood by me like a pillar of strength, I wouldn't be reaching out to all those metaphysical avenues and techniques. I understand that life is all about the imperfections and incompleteness which hold the key to our ultimate calling.' She concluded with her beautiful serene smile, full of compassion and life.

The *wabi-sabi* life. That's what I would like to call the saga of this super-duper kintsugi mom.

Chapter 7

MUJŌKEN NO AI

(Unconditional Love - The Elixir of Life)

*T*his is the breathtaking story of one of my close acquaintances. Widowed at the age of thirty-two with four children to raise and having to bear the legacy of her late husband—a debt of around fifty lakh rupees, Sandra was a totally dilapidated pot to begin with. Twenty years ago, fifty lakhs were not a small amount for a middle-class family.

When her husband, Zack, left for the heavenly abode in a mind-boggling car accident, Sandra stood at the threshold of widowhood and motherhood, not knowing what to do or where to go. With no formal education and no resources to either repay the debts or raise her children, who were all below ten years of age, Sandra felt like a sailor on a boat with no oars in a turbulent sea. She felt cheated by destiny and God.

I remember her wailing at the top of her voice at the funeral of her beloved, 'Why did you cheat me? Why did you go away so soon? How will I live without you?' This was followed by an ear-deafening scream full of rage, 'You have no right to leave me. You promised that we will have a long, beautiful life and we would end up in a classy retirement home when our children leave the nest. Now you leave the nest first. No! You can't go. You cheat! You cheat!' (This is an example of the fight response to stress mentioned in the chapter 'Kenzen')

The entire township wept with her. Zack was a much loved and respected gentleman of the locality. A total philanthropist, he was always there for anyone in need and hence his demise was a sorrowful affair for everyone. Sandra was dragged away from her husband's lifeless body and put to sleep with mild doses of intravenous tranquilisers. There was no other way this widow could be pacified and she would have lost her mind if she had continued with the wailing and screaming anymore.

After the initial shock, Sandra slowly came face to face with reality. She had four little souls to nurture and a mountain-like hurdle to surpass—the big debt left behind by Zack. She could not afford to even mourn the departure of her beloved whom she had met in primary school and married at the tender age of sixteen. Zack had been an integral part of her entire life and she was totally devoted to him. Nobody in the family dared suggest a remarriage—as was the norm in her community—because everyone knew the saga of their eternal love. Sandra would always be Mrs Zack, no matter what.

She took over the reins of her life and embarked upon a journey of real heroism, crushing every other challenge that came along the way. Though her siblings were there to support her, the inner journey and fight were her very own. She left no stone unturned to provide her children with the best education possible. Now all of them are well-settled and happily married. At the age of fifty-two, she is grandmother to five adorable little angels.

I got to observe this courageous lady from my teenage years and always wondered how she managed to keep her child-like innocence and incredible sense of humour throughout her life. How exceptionally well she managed to educate all her four children in premium institutions despite being a school dropout herself was commendable. Even when her health wasn't in the best of conditions, I saw her helping her youngest pregnant daughter to appear for her final year graduation exams. She would accompany her daughter to remote places for the final dissertation and project works and sit with her all through the night massaging her feet or making coffee. And on the graduation day, with the latest grandchild on her lap, this proud grandmother had fulfilled all the promises to her beloved. The four precious stones he left behind had been carved into diamonds and Sandra could finally relax.

I witnessed the proud moments of her life in the photo gallery she kept in her living room. On one occasion, she took me through all those memorable moments—her children's graduation days, baby showers of her daughters and daughters-in-law, and birthday celebrations of her grandchildren. It was beautiful to watch her with tear-filled, proud eyes as she recollected all the milestones of her life.

She was a devout Christian and never ever missed a holy mass or fast. I presume that her staunch belief in God must have been the strength that propelled her, together with her undying love for Zack. However, I always had a lingering fear for her health in the long run. After the youngest daughter's delivery and graduation, I could see the gradual decline in Sandra's health. All the birds had flown out of the nest and though her children and their spouses were extremely caring, there was no purpose for her to pursue. There was nothing more to live for. My fears came true one morning when I woke up to the news that Sandra had a massive heart attack and was posted for immediate bypass surgery.

***

Months later, after the prolonged hospital stay and rest period, I paid a visit to Sandra's house. As we spoke, she asked, 'Haseena, can you give me a homoeopathic medicine to get some sleep? It's been ages since I have slept properly. I don't want to take sleeping pills and get habituated. I already have a handful of medicines after the bypass surgery and I want to reduce or even stop all these Allopathic medicines.'

I looked into those wide, brown eyes I so admired which still had not lost their lustre but there was a lost and hopeless look in them that pulled a string in my heart. I really wished to be of some assistance to this lady whom I respected so much. So, I probed her from the perspective of a homoeopath. She was diabetic, had glaucoma of the eyes, and postmenopausal symptoms as well. The years of suppressed emotions due to being at the giving end of love and care to everyone around had finally got hold of her heart. She felt drained after years of nursing and catering to everyone's needs. Also, since all her children were settled now, she felt that they did not need her anymore.

I prescribed acidum phosphoricum, the drug that would take care of her weakness and entropy of the long years of self-neglect. I assured her that she was going to sleep like a baby and that her heart would never ever go in for another attack. We could also reduce the Allopathic medicines with time. But I knew that what was truly required was for her to pick up the reins of life once again. (For more details, visit: www.materiamedica.info/en/materia-medica/james-tyler-kent/phosphoric-acid)

'Sandra, how did you cope despite losing the one and only love of your life?' I asked to get to her inner core.

'I have never felt that he is not here with me. He is always by my side and that's from where I draw all my energy,' she replied with that look only true lovers have. 'He left his blood and flesh for me to look after and I simply did my duty to perfection. I surrendered everything to God and asked for his guidance whenever I felt totally lost. I staunchly believe that God has bigger plans for all of us because I see how educated and successful my children are now. If Zack was here, we all would have taken life for granted and my children would have wafted in the comfort and luxury Zack always provided. They would have been deprived of the intrinsic need to stand on their own feet and live according to the means of the family.

'Zack was too naïve when it came to money matters and never thought of the future while hoarding us with luxuries beyond our capacity. Being a philanthropist, he never knew how to say "no" to anyone who approached for help and would borrow money or even pawn my jewellery and our other assets to meet their needs. That's how the huge debt built up. If it continued, we would have been on the roads long ago. At that tender age, I did not know how to control or manage him or my family. So, you see, Almighty had to give us this blow to teach us the inevitable lessons of survival and how to have irrefutable faith in him. My children now know how to live within their means and still be compassionate and sensitive to the needs of fellow beings.'

'So, are you happy, Sandra?' I inquired.

'Yes, dear,' she replied. 'I am very happy. I have done all in my power to bring up my children and they are on their own now.'

'So, what are your plans now?' I prodded.

'What plans, Haseena? All duties are done. It is time to go to Zack,' she said, pointing a finger up to heaven.

'So, you are finished with your life at fifty-two?' I asked with an exclamation.

Sandra gave me a curious look. 'What else can I crave for in life? My children no longer need me. I am many times taken for granted. Now I am just the nanny for their children.' I sensed her frustrations slowly brimming up and the forlorn look in her eyes. I could also see that she longed for something more in life—to be really loved and cared for. She had inadvertently said it.

'Life has been a long adventure, Haseena. I won't say that my children don't love me, but once they are married and have their own lives, we single mothers become a burden. How I wish I could reach Zack as soon as possible.'

So that was it! She had given up on life. She needed to feel loved once again to move forward. 'Sandra, at fifty-two, you are at the threshold of an entirely new era of life, post all responsibilities. It is the time to live for yourself and you have already given up on life? What if I suggest marriage, now that you have successfully completed all your duties?' I asked her with some apprehension.

She almost threw the knife at me with which she was cutting an apple, as if I had said something sinful. 'How can you say this, Hasee! I am Zack's wife and will remain so till my death,' she retaliated with fierce-looking eyes.

I could no longer take the conversation forward, even though I clearly perceived the dissatisfaction and grief she was subtly holding on to and the desperate longing for love and validation. I left it at that but nevertheless came away with the satisfaction that I had sowed the seed of a thought in her.

***

Six months passed and one day, Sandra suddenly appeared at my doorstep, alone in a hired taxi, contrary to her usual habit of travelling with her driver and being accompanied by either her daughter-in-law or daughter. The moment I saw her, the transformation was too evident to be ignored. She looked like a freshly-bloomed flower. Her eyes glittered like little bright stars in the sky. Her lips were full and red, and her cheeks were glowing as if she had just come out of the beauty parlour. The tired, diabetic, cardiac patient was nowhere to be seen. Here was a new Sandra; in fact, the old Sandra I knew twenty years ago.

Even before I could utter a single word, she engulfed me in a bear hug, then caught hold of my hand and literally dragged me upstairs to my bedroom, all the way saying, 'Haseena, I have something important to tell you. Let's go to your bedroom. Don't want anyone to hear.'

I was so anxious and impatient to know what she had to say but realised that she was more eager to talk. She closed the bedroom door behind us, settled herself onto my bed, and asked me to sit beside her. She then took out a very beautiful purse with 'Haseena' printed on it and gave it to me.

'What a beauty!' I exclaimed. 'It is custom made for me! Thank you, Sandra.'

I then noted her brand new handbag with 'Sandra' printed on it. The next moment, she held out her palm and on it was the most beautiful ring I had ever set eyes on. It had 'Sandra' carved so beautifully on it. She smiled mischievously like a little girl.

Confused with all this, I asked, 'Have you started some business in customised printing or carving work? They are all incredible works of art, dear. Fantastic!'

She smiled mischievously again, took out her cell phone, and showed me the picture of a middle-aged man, very unassuming in appearance, but with the kindest of eyes and salt and pepper neatly cut beard and hair. I looked at her questioningly. She then narrated to me a story that would put Romeo-Juliet and Laila-Majnu love stories to shame.

It all started after a casual chat on a WhatsApp alumni group of her high school classmates. One of her old friends had asked for her permission to share her phone number with Sid, who was their senior in school. Sandra found nothing wrong in recapturing nostalgic memories with old buddies and readily gave consent. The very next day, Sid called and Sandra was really glad to reminisce with him about their school days. They laughed as they shared jokes and in between, she casually commented, 'Well Sid, your high school heart-throb Liza is happily married with five children. Do you still remember her?'

His answer came as a shock as well as a pleasant surprise. 'Who told you that Liza was my heart-throb? It was always you Sandra. I have been searching for you all over the world from the time we left school. I could never ever forget you. At that age, I was literally terrified to open up because of your two brothers who were always by your side like bodyguards. Your aristocratic, rich family would chop me into pieces had I approached you with a love letter. Liza was my messenger dove, the channel through which I collected all your information. While you would be walking from school with Liza to your house, I would wait by the roadside. Do you remember that Liza and I would gesture to each other? It was all about you Sandra, but you thought we were in love.

'I was so determined to be worthy of you and your aristocratic family and travelled across the globe to become the highly successful businessman that I am now. But before I could approach you with my achievements, you were married to Zack and I came to know that you were extremely happy. I did not want to disturb your tranquil life, so I left India forever and got married to a woman arranged by my parents. I have three girls but have been living the life of an ascetic as my marriage turned out to be a disaster.

'With you in every cell of my existence, I could never ever love my wife, though I did every bit of my duty to perfection. She is still with me and I satisfy all her needs but we have not slept in the same room for the past eight years.' After a small pause, Sid continued, 'I know I should not have told you all this, but I would never die in peace if I did not say this to you at least once in this lifetime, Sandra. I don't wish to disturb your family life and do convey my heartfelt regards to Zack,' he stopped with a sigh.

Sandra was dumbstruck for a long time. Neither did she know of this incredible one-sided saga of love nor did Sid know that she was a widow. Finally, she found her voice and told, 'But Sid, Zack is no more. I have been a widow for twenty years.'

It was now Sid's turn to be dumbfounded. He could not believe his ears. She could literally hear his sobs at the other end of the phone followed by words of compassion and understanding. That moment was like a God-given gift of love she had never expected in this life again.

Their conversation lasted for three hours that day and it had been five months since. Sandra was now on her highway to a collective abundance of love, peace, harmony, and unbounded happiness. Her children were only happy for their mother to have found love once again. All those customised designer accessories were Sid's tokens of love. The purse was his gift for me, Sandra's healer who had coaxed her to accept love when it comes. He calls me Khalil Gibran's sister, jokingly quoting from *The Prophet*, 'When love beckons to you, follow him, and when his wings enfold you, yield to him.'

I had nothing to say as tears of joy were flowing unabated down my cheeks. I could only reach over and hold her in a long hug. We sat in the embrace for a long time, and when we finally disentangled, I probed her more about the future of the relationship. 'Now that you have found love once again, is marriage round the corner? How about his wife?'

Sandra was very clear about her decision. 'No, Hasee,' she said. 'Sid is more than willing to accept me as his wife, but I don't want to disturb the tranquillity and flow of anyone's life just at the moment. Though he is at loggerheads with his wife, he is a man of justice and will never divorce her out of his sense of duty and I don't want him to, as well. Moreover, what will my children, their in-laws, and Zack's family think of me?'

I wondered about the mindset of our Indian women who still put everyone but oneself above everything. They are trained to always live for others, live according to others' opinions, and conform to the norms of society. The 'me' factor comes right at the end. I felt pity as well as a slight irritation towards this attitude of hers.

I pretended to be a little offended and asked, 'Sandra, you have finally found a soulmate after twenty years of widowhood and having completed all your responsibilities as a mother. Why can't you think about your life for just once? Where was this society when you struggled all alone to reach where you are now? Where was this society when you cried for years on your pillow, lying on a cold bed with not a shoulder to lean upon? Where was this society when you were running from door to door to finish off the debts Zack had left behind? Please come out of your trance, dear, and start life anew. Zack would only be happy to see that you are living your life once again.'

Sandra would not be placated. She said, 'Hasee, I am just content to have a soulmate on whom I can always rely. I no longer feel alone. I sleep listening to Sid's voice and wake up to his good morning messages. I feel like a teenager experiencing her first love. I don't want to spoil the beauty and harmony of this life by complicating it with the hassles of marriage, legalising it, and traumatising his wife. I crave no physical intimacy. This flow of love and mutual respect is enough for me to live.' She continued, 'Also, I must tell you that my menses which had stopped one year back have returned and I am getting regular periods since two months.'

I sat in awe, witnessing the beauty that the energy of love can bring to a person. Even her hormones reacted to the miraculous changes that were happening in her brain due to the stimulus of the energy of love. Her happy neurotransmitters, serotonin, oxytocin, and endorphins, were all dancing to the tune of wondrous joy, arousing her feminine energy and stimulating her female hormones to again ovulate and menstruate.

Science cannot explain this phenomenon and no research protocol will suffice to prove these inexplicable events in her life. But living testimonials of the working of this invisible energy of love can neither be denied nor demonstrated with the tools of science. Just as all truths of Mother Nature, the power of the energy of true love is beyond the limits of our comprehension.

What I observed in all cases, including that of Sandra, was that it is either the abundance of love or the lack of it, which is at the root of all experiences in life. You are either in pursuit of love and acceptance which eludes you, attracting all the negative experiences that come with it, or you are basking in the abundance of love which is all-encompassing and, in its wake, attracting positive experiences. Unconditional love without possessiveness is one of the greatest tools to healing.

My take away from this beautiful love story is this: always accept unconditional love coming your way. There is nothing to be guilty of even if you are a single mother or widow of a once-loving husband. No societal norms and pressures need to deter you from your path of peace and happiness. The ultimate goal of every life, humans and animals alike, is to find that reservoir of love and honour your needs. Your children will thank you for being your authentic self. They will learn to be true to themselves when they face life.

Chapter 8

IKIGAI

(The Reason for Your Being)

I was invited to speak to a small crowd of women during the inaugural function of a women-only gym, as part of Women's Day celebrations. The subject was stress management for mom entrepreneurs and it was a beautiful sight to behold. So many young mothers had enthusiastically come forward to pursue their dreams and create their own niches.

This new picture of the conventional Indian society was indeed heartening. The most unique part was that the whole crowd in front of me had their heads covered or had a niqab. It was a welcome change to witness the paradigm shift occurring in the orthodox and conservative outlook of the hitherto Muslim culture in this small province of my state. I was witnessing an entirely novel community of self-motivated, self-sufficient, and empowered women slowly emerging in our patriarchal society.

As I plunged into the usual routine of mutual introductions and icebreakers, I noticed a uniquely dressed girl of about twenty years of age, sitting in the front row responding to every question I asked with very bold answers. She was clothed in a striking pink tracksuit and a sports tee-shirt with a scarf around her hair tied into a ponytail, which made her look even more childlike. Together with the fiery red lipstick and lucid, energetic body language, this girl simply stood out of the crowd. As the session progressed, I learnt that this firecracker was an engineer, thirty-two years old, and a passionate gymnast and fitness enthusiast. She was not representative of the crowd I was speaking to and was there as a fitness consultant to the gym that was being inaugurated.

Somehow the picture of this girl, Zeba, lingered in my mind for many days after the session. Her revolutionary look and the bold decision to be single at thirty-two in a conventional Muslim society (where girls are exclusively brought up to get 'happily married' by the age of twenty at the most) somehow kindled my interest. This girl and her antics stayed with me for weeks, and as destiny would have it, her name kept being repeatedly mentioned by many mutual acquaintances. That was when things fell into place.

Zeba was the daughter of a very ardent women's empowerment activist who was a single mother as well. I am again forced to use the word serendipity because Sara, Zeba's mother, who was also a corporate trainer and motivational speaker, had fascinated me for some time now and I had been wishing to get an interview with her. My aim was to bring out her story for other women wishing to pursue a career in HR training and public speaking; professions rarely taken up by women in my state. But little did I know that she was a single mom warrior and would become the next protagonist to be added to my list of kintsugi moms! It was no wonder that Zeba stood out from the crowd. A daughter raised by an activist and strong single mom could only become a bold and daring person.

Needless to say, I got access to Sara within a few days as part of a social event, and the preordained interview happened over a video call. I was personally quite thrilled about our meeting as Sara's life journey was truly inspiring and she had also agreed to be featured in my book.

As with every story of marital discord, Sara also had the usual narratives of personal incompatibilities with her ex-husband. There was nothing exceptional until she disclosed certain facets of her life that took me by surprise. The fact that she was single by personal choice and the reason she had decided to walk out of her marriage was because Zeba forced her to do so were the most interesting of them. It was no easy task to be single and maintain your dignity as she did in the then social set-up.

Here is Sara's story, without resorting to any more spoilers.

***

Sara was born into a middle-class family in a suburban south Indian province. Her father was a social worker and a small-scale businessman with a heart of gold. He worked for the upliftment of underprivileged women through his small factory and the local governing bodies. Sara would accompany him to his factory and hear about the atrocities women were going through. Domestic abuse, in-law issues, dowry issues, and many other such stories were a common narrative. Sara developed a rebellious attitude towards the existing social norms and became very apprehensive about getting married. All she wanted was to work for the upliftment and empowerment of women. However, the conventional culture and society where she grew up would not allow her to remain single for long. Though her father was immensely supportive in all areas of her life, he would not allow Sara to find her own partner. So, she finally agreed to get married to her brother's friend, Harris, who was supposed to be very progressive and a supporter of women's rights and justice. Thus, it seemed that she would not have to compromise on her dreams to become a social worker. She was busy enrolling for her graduation even while the wedding preparations were going on.

Harris was working abroad while she stayed with his parents in the initial years after their marriage. Her in-laws turned out to be really good souls who supported her in every way. So, when Zeba was born just after thirteen months of marriage, she didn't consider it a big deal as her mother-in-law was there to take care of the child. Harris visited them once a year for a month and thus Sara was blissfully ignorant of his real character until he decided to take her along with him.

Once abroad, Sara had to take on more responsibility as a wife and mother. With no domestic help coming in, life started on an entirely new note. Back at home in India, all household responsibilities rested on her mother-in-law and Sara was a carefree bird enjoying the long-distance relationship with her husband, together with her studies. The one month Harris was at home was like having repeated honeymoons. Problems started when the couple began interacting at close quarters on a daily basis. That is when the gigantic proportions of incompatibilities in their personalities started surfacing. Harris turned out to be an extremely dominating and strict husband with many obsessions and fixations of his own. Sara was expected to live at the end of a tight rope with a set schedule of tasks assigned to her every day. Being a smart girl, she managed to learn the language of the new country very soon. So, the entire responsibility of the house was subtly handed over to her, from going out to the supermarket for groceries, paying the monthly bills, and taking care of the schooling and other needs of Zeba and Salman (their son who was born the next year after she shifted there).

Sara didn't realise the slow change in her while catering to the needs of the family and Harris's haphazard behaviours. He would reprimand her for the smallest of mistakes like leaving the front door keys in the latch or forgetting to switch off the lights in a room. She was cut off from any communication with her relatives in India as the landline, which was the only mode of distant communication at that time, was locked before he left for office and opened only in his presence at night. She was allowed to call home once a week and that too only for a few minutes.

Sara was subtly being tied down to a life of seclusion. The free-spirited rebellious feminist was reduced to a mere puppet in the hands of an obsessive, male chauvinist of a husband. In spite of all this, studies were something she relentlessly pursued, through distance learning programmes. All expenses towards her education were taken care of by her dad and therefore Harris had no choice but to let her continue. Nevertheless, he had a very cunning way of dissuading her from her passion by constantly criticising and frightening her with the dismal status of women in that Arabian country where job opportunities for women even with the best of education were bleak. However, Harris couldn't curtail her thirst for knowledge and soon she became a postgraduate in sociology. So, his next tactic was to prevent her from forming any connections with people. If she tried to build a friendly community in the neighbourhood, he would somehow create petty issues with their spouses and confine Sara to the four walls of the house, except of course when it was time to run errands for the family. Their third child, Milia, was born during this period, which further deprived her of time and energy for herself.

Though the feminist in Sara rebelled to break out of the shell, the mother in her could not. She found it inappropriate to share her woes with her parents or only sister Samia and carried on, curbing all her intrinsic needs. The fiercely independent and rebellious women's rights warrior was slowly withering away until one day, she noticed Harris engaged in a long, French kiss with Zeba. The child was gasping for breath and Sara impulsively pulled her away from his grip. She had heard stories of biological fathers molesting their own children, but even then, she could not believe that Harris would do that to his own daughter and dismissed the incident. She remained in this denial even after he started abusing the youngest daughter, Milia, who was just three years old at the time. He would feed the girls from his lips and bathe them while lingering on their genitals for more than the required time. Zeba, who had grown up by then, could now sense the difference between a fatherly touch and a sinister one. She started secluding herself from everyone which affected her performance at school as well.

Sara sensed that something was amiss, but the conventional mother in her could not accept the fact that her home was a venue for atrocious child abuse and molestation. Harris was a hopeless partner in bed with impotency issues. She had never felt any kind of passionate connection in her sex life with him. In fact, she didn't even know what an orgasm was and hence could not believe that he would be interested in sex or could be a paedophile.

As luck would have it, Sara's sister, Samia, and her family migrated from India to a nearby apartment as her husband had taken up a new job in the country. Zeba, who was very close to her aunt, found excuses to frequently sleep over at their house. Samia was smart enough to pick up on cues and couldn't let the matter go unnoticed. She tactfully made Zeba open up to her. Shocked by the revelation, she immediately informed Sara of the grave situation. This lightning-like exposure to the reality of matters took Sara on a roller-coaster ride of emotional upheavals. She descended into a vicious cycle of self-remorse and guilt for being an irresponsible mother. Her misconstrued notion of the ideal father-daughter relationship had made her blind to the truth of affairs. She blamed herself for being in denial of what was happening right under her nose for years as her helpless daughters were becoming victims of their own father's sexual perversions.

As days passed, Sara's bond with guilt, resentment, and self-reproach grew stronger, and she changed from being a nice, loving, and caring person to an angry, fearful, cantankerous, sad, and extremely secluded person. She was deluding herself that she was a strong woman and could deal with all odds.

On the contrary, she was in a delicate state of mind, unaware of how to react, express, or respond to her erratic thoughts and behaviours. At times, she would contemplate penalising Harris, but ended up doing nothing except shutting herself in a room and weeping for hours. However, she finally found her voice when Zeba threatened to run away from home if she had to live with her father any longer. The desperate girl was at the end of her wits and refused to tolerate any more sexual assaults. Sara realised that divorce was the only option if at all she and her daughters ever hoped to have a normal life. The fact is that it took a little teenager to open her eyes and with Samia's support, Sara embarked upon 'mission separation' in a very subtle manner. She managed to convince Harris to send her and their children to India on the pretext of the lack of good Indian schools to educate their son (Girls' education wouldn't have been a good point to put before him).

Immediately after her arrival in India, she sent a divorce notice to Harris which was naturally met with massive resistance. But in due course, he agreed to sign it on terms of mutual consent, as he knew the grave consequences if Sara dragged the matter to court. He knew that he would be convicted and that would tarnish his reputation forever. Sara also didn't want to take it to court because then the real reason for separation would have to be put on the table and that would bring Zeba into the picture along with the gruelling court procedures and embarrassing questioning. She dreaded the torture her daughter would have to go through.

From an activist or feminist point of view, it was entirely unpardonable to leave that scoundrel unperturbed, but to Sara, nothing mattered except that she had her children safe though emotionally scarred. She did not waste any time trying to bring Harris to justice. She didn't even demand any alimony from him. With the unstinted support of her parents and sister, she started life anew, far away from her hometown, mainly to evade the intruding eyes of the so-called 'compassionate' society.

This was the start of the kintsugi process for Sara. She not only had to mend herself but also her scarred children. After starting over, the immediate need was money, huge amounts of it, for setting up a new home, career, and supporting the education of her three kids. The determination that comes out of desperation and need helped her surpass all hurdles and Sara sprang into action like a superhero and set up an institution in no time. She learnt to process her emotions, align with herself, love herself once again, and overcome the guilt, grief, and loss of dignity as a woman, all of which virtually skyrocketed her approach and attitude towards life.

She recollected the heroic journey of self-repair, 'I used to sit for hours together, devastated between the prospect of life and death, with no resources whatsoever to move on. I cursed myself for opting for the life of a homemaker despite being a graduate. Immediately after separation, I barely managed to enrol my kids in the local schools with my parents' financial support. With nothing to do till they returned from school in the evening, I started wandering in the unfamiliar city to ward off the utter sense of loneliness. It was also like a rebellion, a break to freedom after the years of slavery I had been subjected to by Harris. These wanderings took me to the nearby parks, orphanages, old-age homes, ashrams, and mosques. I started attending literary functions and took the help of self-help books and attended transformational workshops. With every book I read, I peeled layers of negativity and pain from within. I continued to do it until I could make peace with myself, and life. In the process, rather than looking outward, I learnt to find closure within.'

She went through many months of introspection and processes to emerge as the wonder woman she is called now.

She triumphed at providing a nourishing and nurturing environment for her children and educated them in the best universities. All three of them have become successful professionals with a die-hard attitude and clear outlook on life and relationships, much like their mother.

Zeba, at thirty-two, still has reservations about marriage and men due to her bitter experiences, yet she is waiting for the right partner to manifest. She is lucky enough to have a mother like Sara who has given her all the freedom to live the way she wants, whether in wedlock, in a living-together relationship, or as a single independent woman. She is also an ardent fighter for women's rights. Though Sara and her kids are a sore eye to the conventional orthodoxy, they are beautiful kintsugied pots to the world out there, inspiring hundreds with their words and life experiences.

＊＊

At the end of the two-hour-long interview, I was left with no alternative but to admire the courage and resilience of this warrior mom. There was nothing that I could have offered to her as a healer. Instead, I imbibed wisdom and insights from her, which I decided to put forth for all my readers. I needed one more profound insight to conclude this incredible story and hence asked, 'Why do you think your life became so, Sara? Do you think this was your destiny and you unconsciously attracted such a life to get you to your ambition of being a social worker?'

She smiled and replied, 'Yes, exactly doc. I was always ambitious. My goal in life was to become a stalwart for the empowerment of women. The stories of the downtrodden women in my father's factory had sown the seed for it. I had seen my mother cry when overwhelmed with domestic responsibilities. Even though my father was a very good soul, he had no time for her, due to social and financial responsibilities. After witnessing all this, I developed a very negative attitude about marriage and men and by default, I attracted such a man into my life, reproducing the mental picture of my childhood beliefs.

'Little things like forgetting keys on the front door or making Harris irritated by my absent-mindedness were the cons I was leaving unconsciously to provoke the bad side of him to ultimately get my point right at the end of the day. Even the sexual abuse he subjected our children to was a replay of what I had heard in our village, though in a different context. I was subconsciously replaying all the childhood memories in my life.

'After all the inner work I did after taking the most difficult decision of separation and the struggles to raise my children, I take total responsibility for my life and even thank Harris for being in my life to finally get me anchored to my purpose.' She continued, 'I was always a truly free-spirited woman and my role-playing of a submissive, perfect homemaker was a façade that could not last long, though fifteen years was too long a time I took to fathom the cowardly existence that I was leading. Now I have learnt to forgive and forget everything. I have forgiven Harris for all that he did. I have forgiven myself for being in self-denial about what Zeba and Milia were going through. Now my family is a bunch of bubbling, happy souls, sailing in a boat of never-ending peace, joy, and sublime bliss.

'The only drawback of being single is the constant pressure of the world around to get me married again and hence my forced inhibition to freely interact with any prospective single or separated middle-aged men.' She smiled and continued, 'I am very clear about my life purpose and I need no man to complete myself. I am not made for matrimony and the adjustments and compromises it calls for. I live life on my terms. Yes, I have limitations while travelling alone in India, which has become an increasingly unsafe place for women.

Yet, I am not willing to compromise my freedom to have the so-called security of being in wedlock. I know I am enough to protect myself. All three of my children are also trained in martial arts and all other means to protect themselves. I say children because nowadays even boys are not immune to sexual assaults. Therefore, for me, it is not just about women's rights; it is about human rights, irrespective of sex.'

Hearing her profound life observation and insight, I was reminded of a book, *I Can See Clearly Now*, by Wayne W. Dyer where he explains how everything in life happens for a reason. But my curiosity was still not satiated and so I asked, 'Sara, one final, very personal question, which if not asked will not complete my survey and interview. Haven't you craved for a sexual partner and that intimacy ever?'

'Who does not crave for human touch and sex, Haseena? I am a perfectly normal woman with all the basic instincts. It is just that I don't consider it worthwhile to sacrifice the more important part of my existence for that alone,' she boldly admitted. 'I enjoy masturbation once in a while and feel powerful by myself. I have never thought that I needed to enter an obligatory relationship with any man to satisfy my bodily needs. Now as menopause is nearing, the urge is also gone and I am perfectly at peace with my body and soul. I do my workouts, have a gala time with my kids, and have ample time with myself and my girlfriends, travelling around the world as part of my workshops and holidays.'

Sara's life is an example of how everything in life reveals itself in time to teach the reason for your being, your *ikigai*.

I am sharing below a beautiful poem written by a close friend of mine, Shahnaz, which vividly portrays Sara's indomitable free spirit and self-pride and is also a warning to every man who thinks he can take advantage of single women.

We, The Unit (Single and Complete)

Be nice
Just as we are,
Be friends, if you can be.
Do not help, do not take over,
Do not be the man at our service
Just be nice
And let us be.
Don't understand us to be lonely and sad,
Or bored
And definitely free.
In fact, we're the busiest as we do things
Our own
And we're happier than your wives and
Not so lonely as your old mothers
And married sisters.
If you have so much time
Be there for them.
Our freedom is our elixir for life
And we would trade that for nothing.
To you, we may seem complicated,
Selfish, heartless,
Yes, we are selectively so.
Just be friends if you can and if you want!
If you expect benefits
You're not fit to be one.
Don't force us time and again to
Make rudeness our virtue.

SECTION 2

Overview

As we come to the end of the chronicles of courage and resilience, I thank you, my dear reader, for travelling with me and my kintsugi moms. Since you have reached this far in the book, it is obvious that it was not by chance but by choice that you are here and that you are in search of those golden nuggets to fill in the crevices of the broken parts of either yourself or someone you know. Hope the next few pages, which contain a cornucopia of healing tools, will help you mend those scars and make them adornments to be proud of.

Out of hundreds of stories in my case diary, I have selected only the relevant ones for this book; those which encompassed challenges that needed to be addressed from different perspectives of healing. In this section, we will consolidate everything hitherto discussed to get a general picture of the essential healing challenges faced by single mothers and the ways to confront them.

Broadly speaking, most of the challenges for single moms come from the social, psychological, and physical realms. The myriad of societal pressures that leaves a single mother overwhelmed and haggard at the end of the day are diverse. Alienation, non-acceptance, ostracisation, and conflicts pertaining to sex, dating, and remarriage are some of the major social challenges she has to face. Add to these the preying eyes and illicit approaches of some perverted men folk, and life becomes unbearable.

There are single moms who told me how difficult it is to survive even in a professional setting because they were taken for granted as easy prey for sexual advances. Solo travel becomes a herculean task. 'If you happen to disclose that you are a single mother even during a casual conversation, the attitude changes and you are made to feel like an alien from some remote planet,' said one of my clients. Some react with sympathy while some get sarcastic, both of which are totally unacceptable. Also, attacks and suggestive remarks on social media handles mostly force single mothers to go into seclusion.

In the Indian subcontinent—mostly in rural North India—single moms, especially widows, are considered a bad omen and alienated from auspicious family functions. There are cases where they were rejected rented houses and even ousted from residential communities simply because of their marital status. It is also not uncommon for neighbours and relatives to constantly pry into their personal lives and gossip about everything they do with a preconceived malicious outlook. Their children are subjected to isolation on the false account that single-parented children are bound to be spoilt and would be a bad influence on their so-called 'normal bred' counterparts.

Unsolicited advice from every Tom, Dick, and Harry, legal issues, and financial and career pressures are just a few of the other challenges a single mom has to face on an external level. But even more devastating are the internal demons and their physical implications.

Internal demons take the form of psychological challenges of varied hues and intensity. Insecurity, fear, loneliness, anxiety, sadness, depression, anger/mania, guilt, resentment, loss of confidence and self-esteem, feeling of self-doubt and inadequacy of her capabilities as a parent, etc. are some of the major issues that plague single mothers.

These psychological stresses many a time affect their physical health and can manifest as multifarious ailments like migraine, hypertension, diabetes, thyroid and other hormonal disorders, auto-immune disorders, diseases of the breast, ovary, or uterus, irritable bowel syndrome, fibromyalgia, and cancer, to name a few.

This invariably takes us to the next question: What are the ways to heal them? Many of the strategies have been dealt with in the previous chapters. Here we will discuss each of them more elaborately, so that you get an idea as to how to adapt them according to your personal needs.

A word of caution before moving on, my dears. Kindly note that the tools mentioned and explained in different chapters of this book were effective for that particular person in consideration. There is no one-size-fits-all approach or solution when tackling complex mental and physical issues. What resonates with one person's constitution and issues may not resonate with another. For instance, I have read an umpteen number of self-help books and attended numerous seminars and workshops on various healing modalities but not all of them resonated with me. So, my dear reader, it is up to you to imbibe and assimilate only those techniques that you feel would necessarily benefit you. For that, you need to first identify your individual issues and customise the tools to your advantage. I can nevertheless assure you that if followed with faith and conviction, all the techniques outlined have the potential to quicken your journey towards total healing.

So, let us recapitulate the tools and techniques for healing one by one.

Chapter 1

THE ROAD MAP TO KINTSUGI

(The Art of Transmuting Your Scars into Adornments)

From the stories depicted here and many others, it is obvious that at the core of every situation in life is love. Love is the most powerful energy, the lack of which can break you and the abundance of which can make you. As I said in Maria's story, we are all in pursuit of love and acceptance and search for it everywhere except in ourselves.

We have seen that all the protagonists in our stories were broken to begin with. At some point in their respective journeys, they got in touch with their inner selves. You may call it a spiritual calling or awakening, but ultimately, there comes a turning point, an 'aha' moment, from where these women start fixing themselves. They learn to love themselves and take a U-turn to wholeness and self-transformation. They reach the point of realisation that everything in life happened for their ultimate good and this propels them to become icons of peace and tranquillity.

So, you see that learning to truly love and accept yourself forms the crux of the kintsugi process. However, self-love isn't a magic fix for financial insecurity, depression, anxiety, exhaustion, loneliness, or resentment. But it does offer a foundation for being the best version of yourself and to become a better parent as well.

When you learn to love yourself, you start to take responsibility for your life. You realise that there is no point in blaming yourself or your past, including your ex-partners who you think did not do justice to you. You understand that it takes two to make a quarrel, meaning that either consciously or unconsciously, you have also contributed to the situation. This culminates in the realisation that there are no accidents in the universe. Each and every circumstance and individual in your life is what you have called forth by your thoughts and belief systems. You understand that they all were in your life to teach you the lessons you needed to reach your ultimate purpose. This opens an entirely new world of infinite possibilities. You embrace forgiveness and unconditional love to reach that coveted hub of true enlightenment.

As James Allen says in his book, *As a Man Thinketh*, 'You need to realise that the circumstances in your life are the direct consequences of your thoughts and belief systems. Man is made or unmade by himself. In the armoury of thought, he forges the weapons by which he destroys himself. He also fashions the tools with which he builds for himself heavenly mansions of joy and strength and peace.'

I can vouch for these insights being a single mom myself. I have been separated for the last sixteen years but still hold a very amicable relationship with my ex-husband, who has remarried and has a daughter. I also share a beautiful relationship with my ex-mother-in-law who still comes to stay with my son and me. When our relationship didn't work even after ten years of togetherness, I didn't think it prudent to get into the vicious circle of resentment and mud-slinging. We had a common factor, our son, and we both wanted the best for him. So, we chose to co-parent him whilst leading our individual lives. In the end, we are all happy, peaceful, and co-exist with mutual respect and love for each other. I know that he came to my life to teach me the lessons I needed to complete my sojourn on this earth. But this realisation didn't come in one day. I had my own set of challenges to overcome. I went into depression for many months post our separation. There were so many unbearable moments of grief, fear, insecurity, and resentment but all that took me deeper into the realities of life, which ultimately led me to the sublime peace and tranquillity that I was searching for. I had to hit rock bottom to finally reach out and learn my lessons in self-love. I then realised what my soul's purpose was and started attracting exactly what I needed for its fulfilment.

As life progressed, I also realised that one cannot attract a different life unless and until you resonate with the frequencies of your desired outcomes. You cannot just dream and expect that the law of attraction will bring it to you. You must become the change you want to see around you to really attract your dream life. You need to change your mindsets and feel deserving of everything good in the universe, for the simple reason that you exist. You need to believe that you are the most magnificent being you have ever known. Let's take a closer look at what this implies. For example, you cannot wish to be wealthy on one side, and on the other side believe that you don't deserve it because you are not educated enough. Then you go on accepting mundane jobs and wages. To become wealthy, you need to believe that you deserve money and work towards it mentally, physically, and emotionally. Only then will you find opportunities and abundance manifesting from sources you have never ever imagined.

Similarly, you cannot hope to reduce your weight while eating junk food three times a day. Once your intention is clear, you need to first accept yourself as you are and be willing to change yourself to achieve your goal. Then you will automatically develop better food habits and routines. You will no longer consume anything that will go against your intention of attaining your ideal weight and your addictions will also start vanishing on their own.

You need to first love yourself to even attract your true soulmate. You may have had multiple failures in relationships, you may have married more than once, yet in the end, find yourself single. This was the story of one of my clients from Italy. As I probed into her childhood, I found that her stepfather was an alcoholic and used to sexually abuse her from six years of age. She got into the habit of masturbation at that early age as her sexual instincts were aroused much before puberty. At that time, she didn't know what she was doing and by the time she realised it, the damage was already done. She grew up with the feeling that she is impure and not good enough for a man. She condemned herself for masturbating even while she had partners, yet it became like an addiction or obsession. Her belief that she was not worthy of a good man led to each of them abandoning her eventually. She is still in search of a true relationship even at the age of forty-six. I had to educate her that she needed to forgive herself and make a shift in her attitude. For that, she needed to love and accept herself, release all those feelings of guilt, and realise that she was worthy of true love. She has to first become the loving person she wishes to manifest, as only love can attract love.

There was another single mother from Australia—a practising psychiatrist—who attended one of my online workshops on self-love. She had a massive inferiority complex and zero self-esteem due to her obesity and short stature. Though she looked graceful and exotic with her dusky complexion and plump-baby-like countenance, she considered herself the ugliest person on earth. As the workshop progressed, we went into the inner child analysis where she disclosed the reason for this very negative attitude. Her father, a fair, tall man himself, would always compare her negatively with her fairer and slimmer sibling all through her formative years. He openly discriminated between them even in the show of his affection. Hence, even after being an accomplished psychiatrist and doing commendable work among teenage drug abusers, she continued to struggle in her personal life.

She never got the attention of good-looking guys in school or college as she never made herself available, always hiding behind books and academics. She was later married off to a man who turned out to be more abusive and dysfunctional than her father. One night, after a drunken debauch, he even attempted to kill their two-year-old daughter. She had to point a knife and threaten to murder him before escaping with the toddler. They spent the whole night in the car on a lonely roadside until the police reached and found them a shelter. Twelve years later, she was still struggling alone to make ends meet and living in a one-bedroom apartment with her teenage daughter. She was still rejected by every man who entered her life, in spite of being a successful psychiatrist and having a very pleasing personality.

There is no wonder why she was in this fix. How could she attract love when she could not love herself for who she was? After doing the healing modules of self-love online, she started to change little by little. After the five-week course, she called to say that a genuine man had asked her out for dinner. The relationship has become serious is what I understood from our last call and I am eagerly waiting for a magnificent outcome soon. When she learnt to love herself, love started finding her.

So, my dear, if you find yourself not fully satisfied and happy about everything happening around you, understand that you are attracting it by your sense of lack and feeling of unworthiness. Invariably, you are sabotaging your own good as you have lost touch with yourself. Learning to undo all your negative beliefs and love yourself as you are, every crazy bit of it, is integral to healing yourself at all levels. Give yourself the same care and love that you show your children. Understand that self-love is not akin to selfishness or vanity. Instead, it encompasses positive self-care, self-esteem, self-image, and self-determination. Above all, it means taking good care of the person deep inside you. Now, let us see how to get about this business of self-love.

***

'In a strong body dwells a strong mind.'

A fundamental step towards self-love is emotional and physical healing. Understanding and healing your own pain is the ultimate expression of self-love. When you ignore or numb your psychological pains, well-being eludes you. Protecting your physical health is equally important, if not more. Your body and mind require constant repair, rejuvenation, and replenishment. You need to periodically detoxify the inner environment; a sort of mental and physical house-cleaning. Throwing away all the unwanted toxins into the trashcan and replacing them with new ways of thinking and acting is how you make positive changes in life.

It is important to design a purposeful way of living that incorporates daily rituals and long-term strategies that are self-affirming. You deserve it! It will make you a wonderful role model for people around you and equip you to handle the inevitable challenges that come your way. From the story of Vydehi in the chapter 'Kenzen', you know the pathways by which you fall ill and how stress at any level can derange the functioning of your body. So, the first scar to be repaired is the temple in which you have to reside for one long lifetime—your body. Acquiring the tools to ensure the adequate supply of immunity-boosting hormones and enzymes in your body is the first prerequisite for a healthy body and mind.

Let us explore the tools to lasting well-being which I have curated from my personal experiences and first-hand verification by my clientele. Each of the strategies discussed here can run into volumes and hence it is next to impossible to incorporate them into the constraints of this small book. Neither do I consider myself to be a master of all of them nor appear to be pontificating about subjects that I am not fully versed with. I have only tried to give some pointers which you can explore further from the links and references given and also from the vast ocean of visual and auditory material at your fingertips, thanks to technology.

I have classified the tools of self-repair into seven lessons for easy reference:

1. Diet/Nutrition and Fasting
2. Exercise and Breathwork
3. Relaxation and Recreation
4. Sex and Relationships
5. Spirituality and Meditation
6. Taming the Subconscious

    i. Affirmations and Visualisations
    ii. Mirror Work
    iii. Gratitude Journaling
    iv. Inner Child Analysis
    v. Forgiveness
    vi. Emotion Processing
    vii. Ho'oponopono Technique

7. Therapeutic Interventions

Lesson 1: Diet/Nutrition and Fasting

To cover the topic of diet and nutrition, a subject which took me two years of postgraduate study to master, would require a book in itself. However, I have tried to bring out the significant points to keep in mind while taking care of your diet and regimen.

Indian mothers usually start neglecting their health and body after childbirth. This is one reason that post-partum obesity has become so common. Add to it the stresses of a strained relationship/widowhood and single parenting, it is but natural that self-care goes out of the window. Exhaustion and lack of self-care often go hand in hand. But burning the candle at both ends over a long-term period is a risky strategy because it compromises your parenting skills as well. Therefore, you need to overhaul your lifestyle and habits to begin with.

While revamping your habits, an achievable target of a good diet and regimen is mandatory. Your initial goal should be to maintain your ideal body weight and body mass index (BMI). Roughly stated, the ideal body weight is your height in centimetres minus one hundred. For example, if you are 163 cm in height, then your ideal body weight is 163-100=63 kg. So, your targeted weight should be around 63 kilograms. This should be the first parameter while planning your meals and workout schedules.

BMI provides the measure of body fat based on your height and weight. It is calculated by taking the body mass (weight) in kilograms and dividing it by the square of the height in metres. For example, if you are 65 kg in weight and 1.6 metres in height, your BMI would be $65/1.6^2 = 25.4$. The normal range is between 18 and 25. A BMI above 25 indicates obesity and below 18 indicates underweight.

From this starting point, we take upon a journey of repairing and rebuilding ourselves on a daily basis. As we all know, the cells, which are replaced regularly in our body, are phagocytosed and eliminated through the outlets of our body—as urine and stools through the excretory system and as sweat through the skin pores. We call this process metabolism and it requires energy, which we denote by the term calories. It is calculated that an average Indian woman requires 2,200 kilocalories of energy to carry out her daily activities. At any given point in time, our health and well-being depend on the energy which is available to carry out the processes of metabolism. A perfect balance of this energy is what makes us who we are. This energy comes from the food we eat. Therefore, the food we consume should give us optimum nutrition to carry out the metabolic activities of the body along with a strong immune system.

A balanced and systematic diet is the key to optimum nutrition and this comes from what we call nutrients present in food in the form of carbohydrates, proteins, fats, minerals, vitamins, and dietary fibre. A perfect blend of all the nutrients is necessary for the proper functioning of all the physiological and biochemical processes by which the human body acquires, assimilates, and utilises food to maintain health and activity.

Carbohydrates, fats, and proteins which are needed in large amounts, belong to the category of macronutrients. Vitamins and minerals constitute the micronutrients and are required only in smaller amounts. They are supplied by the basic five food groups, namely:

1. Cereals and related products
2. Pulses and legumes
3. Milk and meat products
4. Fruits and vegetables
5. Fats and sugars

Basic Five Food Groups	
Food Groups	**Nutrients**
1. Cereal and related products: Rice, wheat, ragi, maize, millet, rice flakes, wheat flour, oats, muesli, millets, etc.	Protein, invisible fat, B vitamins, iron, calcium, and fibre.
2. Pulses and legumes: Bengal gram, black gram, cowpea, peas, soya beans, lentils, dals, etc.	Protein, invisible fat, thiamine, riboflavin, folic acid, calcium, iron, and fibre
3. Milk and meat products: i. Milk, cheese, curd, etc. ii. Chicken, liver, fish, egg, meat, etc.	Protein, fat, riboflavin, and calcium.
4. Fruits and vegetables: i. Mango, guava, papaya, orange, sweet lime, watermelon, apple, etc. ii. Green leafy vegetables: Amaranth, celery, spinach, drumstick leaves, coriander leaves, fenugreek leaves, etc. iii. Other vegetables: Carrot, onion, brinjal, ladies' fingers, beans, capsicum, cauliflower, drumstick, cabbage, broccoli, potato, etc.	Carotenoids, vitamin C, riboflavin, folic acid, iron, and fibre. Riboflavin, folic acid, calcium, fibre, iron, and carotenoids. Carotenoids, folic acid, calcium, and fibre.
5. Fats and sugars: i. Fats: Butter, ghee, groundnut oil, coconut oil, hydrogenated fat, olive oil, cooking oils, etc. ii. Sugar and jaggery.	Essential fatty acids and fat-soluble vitamins. Iron.

A blend of ingredients from all the food groups, as advocated by the international and national bodies like ICMR or WHO, is highly important for a balanced diet. This was earlier illustrated by the Food Pyramid but it has been replaced by a new concept called the Food Plate which was popularised by Ms Michelle Obama in the US and is now accepted worldwide. It recommends the rainbow concept of food on your plate, which means that all colours of vegetables, fruits, and other foods are to be mixed to get the complete nutrition in each meal. The basic rule is that your plate should have five portions, of which fifty per cent should be fruits and vegetables of various colours, twenty-five per cent should be whole grains, and the remaining twenty-five per cent should be proteins (of both animal and plant origin). This should be accompanied by healthy fats, like vegetable oils and ghee, in moderation and lots of water (two to three litres).

Rainbow Concept of Food Plate

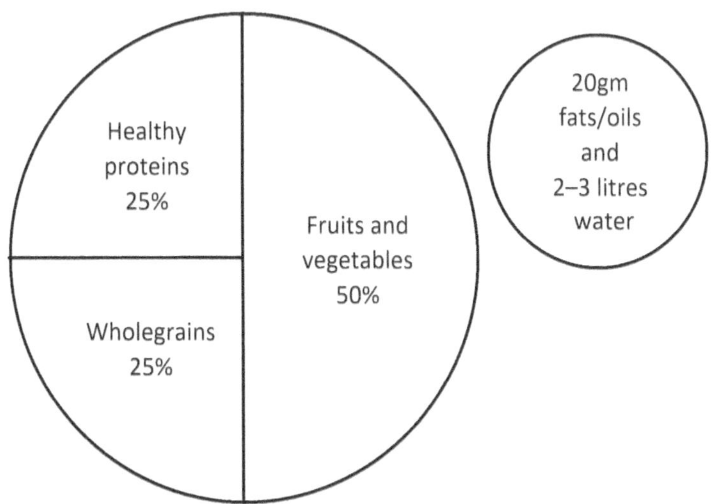

The WHO suggests that at least fifty per cent of calories in our diet should come from complex carbohydrates and no more than thirty-five per cent should come from fat and up to fifteen per cent from protein. The allowance for alcohol consumption is no more than five per cent. The food plate satisfies these criteria of the WHO.

The sources of all the nutrients are demonstrated (see page 161) for your reference. You may customise your diet based on it. However, it is essential that you get aware of the basic needs of your body before deciding on your diet and regimen. From whatever point you begin with a new way of nutrition, it is important to get your health status assessed by a professional. If you have specific health issues like diabetes, hypertension, hypercholesteremia, or any chronic disease, your dietary requirements need to be adapted accordingly, under the strict guidance of a clinical nutritionist/physician.

A balanced diet with a systematic regimen of periodic fasting forms the perfect recipe for a totally healthy body.

Now, what is fasting? It is a practice that dates back centuries and plays a central role in many cultures and religions. Fasting means abstinence from all or some foods or drinks for a set period of time. It has many health benefits ranging from weight loss to better brain function, improved blood sugar and pressure control, and a better balance of triglycerides and cholesterol levels. Fasting can delay ageing, extend longevity, and help decrease levels of inflammation. It also lowers the risk of many chronic diseases like coronary heart disease, neurodegenerative disorders, Alzheimer's disease, Parkinson's disease, and even cancer.

There are different types of fasting methods unique to different cultures across the world and invariably all are conducive to better health and prevention of diseases. Water fasting, juice fasting, intermittent fasting, and partial fasting are some of the prevalent ones. Having said that, I do not recommend any kind of fad diets or fasting methods to my

Nutrient	Sources
Complex carbohydrates and fibre	Whole wheat bread, wholegrain cereals (rice, wheat, millets, etc.), beans, pasta, potatoes, peas, and other starchy vegetables.
Protein	Lean meat, chicken, fish, cheese, milk, eggs, nuts, and legumes.
Fat	Oils, butter, margarine, cream, meat, cheese, ghee, and nuts.
Preformed Vitamin A	Butter, margarine, cream, cheese, eggs, and meat.
Beta-carotene (converts to vitamin A)	Carrots, spinach, pumpkin, broccoli, tomatoes, apricots, and melon.
Vitamin D	Fatty/canned fish, butter, margarine, cream, cheese, and eggs.
Vitamin E	Polyunsaturated oils, polyunsaturated margarine, nuts, olive oil, fatty fish, wholegrain cereals, and green vegetables.
Vitamin K	Green vegetables, cheese, butter, pork, and eggs.
Thiamin	Wholegrain cereals, pork, bread, nuts, and peas.
Riboflavin	Milk, meat, eggs, cheese, wholegrain cereals, nuts, and mushrooms.
Niacin	Fish, meat, peanuts, wholegrain cereals, nuts, and mushrooms.
Pantothenic acid	Eggs, wholegrain cereals, peanuts, fish, meat, and vegetables.
Vitamin B6	Wholegrain cereals, meat, fish, peanuts, and bananas.
Folic acid	Green vegetables, wholegrain cereals, wholemeal bread, and nuts.
Vitamin B12	Meat, fish, eggs, cheese, milk, and oysters.
Biotin	Eggs, cheese, milk, fish, and wholegrain cereals.
Vitamin C	Oranges, tomatoes, potatoes, broccoli, cabbage, brussels sprouts, and strawberries.
Calcium	Cheese, milk, yoghurt, canned fish, nuts, sesame seeds (tahini), and dried fruit.
Phosphorus	Meat, fish, poultry, eggs, milk, cheese, nuts, cereals, and bread.
Iron	Meat, poultry, wholegrain cereals, whole wheat bread, and eggs.
Sodium	Table salt, meat, milk, cheese, seafood, spinach, and celery.
Potassium	Potatoes, bananas, oranges, apricots, fruit, vegetable, meat, fish, and nuts.
Iodine	Seafood, milk and cereals, iodised table salt, and vegetables from areas with high iodine content in the soil.
Zinc	Oysters, meat, fish, poultry, eggs, wholegrain cereals, and peanuts.

clients except for a particular form of diet/fasting which I use for therapeutic purposes only. It is called mono dieting.

It was during my tryst with the initial stage of cancer of the uterus that I came upon the concept of mono dieting in the epoch-making book called *Fit for Life* by Harvey Diamond which changed my attitude towards food and diet forever. I practised every word in the book for about six months and the miraculous results have lasted till now, fifteen years later.

Mono dieting is a unique system of diet/fasting where you are allowed to eat only one type of uncooked natural food at a time so that the body takes minimum energy for the digestive mechanism whilst using the remaining energy to repair the other systems of the body. Let's say, if you decide on vegetables, for one full day, you can have only raw vegetables and vegetable juices with no added sugar. The same goes for fruits. You are not allowed to take any cooked or artificial food or even foods belonging to other groups on that day. You can eat as much as you want on your fasting days and should never feel tired or hungry. You can replenish yourself every two hours and if needed, even more frequently if your body calls for it. A great feature of this diet is that it neither taxes your body nor deprives you of the joy of eating. It strengthens the immune system and washes all toxins out of the body, opening new channels of vitality and good health. (For more information visit: www.vpnutrition. com) I advocate mono dieting to my clients for three days a week during the period of therapy. Once the healing process is over, I ask them to continue with mono dieting once a fortnight throughout life.

A word of caution: Always keep in mind the types of fruits and vegetables you include in your mono diet. They must be selected only after carefully considering all your health parameters. For example, a diabetic patient is never advised to eat too many mangoes or bananas which are rich in direct sugars and may elevate his/her blood glucose levels. On the other hand, completely cutting down on all sweet fruits is also not advisable because it can lead to hypoglycemia. Hence, a diabetic person should take a vegetable diet or eat fruits that are not too sweet. They can consume dry fruits like prunes and dates and even have pure natural honey in moderation to maintain their glucose levels. In between, unsweetened juices rich in minerals, like coconut water and lime juice, can be consumed to ward off fatigue or dehydration.

I have always been fascinated by the Japanese way of life. The book called *Ikigai*, written by Hector Garcia and Francesc Miralles, explores the secrets behind the longevity and happy life of people in Okinawa, a remote village in Japan. Their routine consists of eating wholesome nutritious food five days a week interspersed by fasting for two days. This summarises their secret to a long and healthy life.

Here are some other important dos and don'ts regarding nutrition that I have adapted from various sources over the years:

1. Eat a wide variety of foods available locally instead of looking out for special or wonder foods to bring about some fancy outcome. Explore the roots of your culture and geography and consume food accordingly. For example, while the south Indians have a very balanced food pattern for breakfast which usually consists of idli/dosa, sambhar, milk, tea, and plantain, westerners have their own version of a balanced breakfast which consists of cereal, bacon, milk, egg, and fruits. Both patterns satisfy all the carbohydrate, protein, and vitamin requirements to kick start a day. So, the thumb rule is to imbibe the cultural and traditional cuisine of your area and plan your diet based on it.

2. Though the WHO and ICMR recommend an average of 2,000-2,200 kcal of energy from a day's meal, it is

interesting to note that the people from the Japanese island, Okinawa, consume only about 1,800 kcal per day. They never eat till their stomach is full to the brim. They stop eating the moment they start to feel full, roughly satisfying only eighty per cent of their hunger and thus leaving space for a little more. This routine accelerates the digestive process and metabolism.

3. Base the major part of your diet on natural foods and avoid all seasoned, artificial, refined, and packed or preserved food items. As Louise L. Hay puts it, 'Eat whatever grows.'

4. Avoid white foods like refined sugar, refined flour/ grains, refined salt, and processed dairy products. Instead, go for wholegrain cereals like brown rice and wheat and natural sweeteners like jaggery and honey.

5. Avoid deep-fried and oily foods.

6. While starchy food is necessary to balance the carbohydrate requirements in the body (rice, potato, tubers, etc.), be cautious of their intake quantity. Avoid too much of tubers and rice.

7. Eat plenty of protein-rich foods from both animal and plant sources. Though the Indian concept of *sattvic*, *rajasic*, and *tamasic* foods recommends plant origin proteins over animal proteins, it is not applicable in all countries and to all cultures. A blend of fish, eggs, and lean meat are easy options to satisfy your protein requirements interspersed with vegetable proteins like legumes, nuts, and seeds.

8. Eat at least five to six servings of fruits and vegetables every day. Try to include fruits and vegetables containing a lot of fibre, like green, leafy vegetables and citrus fruits. Have salads of every colour (yellow, green, red, orange, and purple) before each main meal

so that your calories come from natural food while cutting down on empty and harmful calories. Avoid sweetened sieved fruit juices and desserts altogether.

9. Hydrate yourself throughout the day. Have an average of about two to three litres of fluids (not just plain water). Avoid all carbonated and sweetened drinks and use alcohol to a bare minimum. If at all it is unavoidable, have it in the form of natural wine. 'Eat your water' is an interesting metaphor. It means eating fruits and vegetables rich in water content such as melons, cucumber, tomatoes, oranges, etc. Avoid juicing and sieving fruits and vegetables as it takes away most of the nutrients and fibre content. Every time you feel a hunger pang, get a glass of water instead of popping in some snack. Often, we mistake thirst for hunger and this is one of the main causes of obesity and many other physical ailments.

10. Eat lots of antioxidant-rich food. Antioxidants are molecules that slow the oxidation process in cells, which neutralises a substance called free radicals that cause damage to cells. Green tea, citrus fruits, apricots, berries, garlic, oily fish like sardines, mackerels, and tuna, vegetables like broccoli, dried fruits like dates and prunes, and whole grains such as oats and wheat are rich sources of antioxidants.

11. Choose healthy fat, limit saturated fat, and avoid trans-fat. Examples of healthy fat or unsaturated fats are vegetable oils, nuts, and seeds. Saturated fats are found in butter, ghee, cheese, red meats, deep-fried foods, and processed meats. Trans fats are present in baked and processed foods like cookies, cakes, and fried chips.

12. Include foods rich in omega-3 fatty acids like seafood. Seafood is also the richest source of iodine which is necessary for thyroid health. Iodine deficiency is one of the most common causes of goitre and can also lead to congenital defects in offsprings of mothers suffering from it.

13. Include probiotic-rich foods like yoghurt and buttermilk in your diet along with fermented meals like idli and dosa as they enhance the gut flora.

Tips for a Healthy Eating Pattern

1. Start your day with water and a fruit. Never skip breakfast. Have it before 9 a.m.

2. Make sure that every main meal has a combination of carbohydrates, proteins, and micronutrients but try to make dinner completely free of carbohydrates. Instead, opt for a meal that primarily consists of proteins (meat, fish, nuts, legumes, eggs, etc.) and salads (vegetables and fruits). Ideally, have dinner between 7-8 p.m.

3. Instead of three big meals, which leave you satiated and full to the brim, break your meal portions into five or six small meals so that the digestive system is neither overtaxed nor starved for too long. Plan your diets in such a way that the intervals between meals are between two and a half to three hours at the most.

4. Close your kitchen after 8 p.m.

By adopting the above suggestions in your diet and fasting at least one to two days a week, you are bound to bounce back to your natural healthy state. Ensure that you spend a little time with nature and the sun as vitamin D deficiency syndrome is becoming a global epidemic, which is the dismal outcome of our closed indoor lifestyle. Sunlight is the best source of natural vitamin D, the most essential vitamin to assimilate and maintain our calcium levels. Our skeletal system and teeth depend on this vitamin, and it also has far-reaching consequences on our total mental and physical well-being.

Points to Remember When You Enter Your Kitchen

1. When having sea fish, be very particular to eat it entirely. We usually discard the head portion and consume the fleshy body parts but iodine, which is essential to prevent goitre, is mostly concentrated in the upper part of the fish.

2. When having garlic, one of the most important antioxidant-rich foods, crush it raw and allow it to be in the air for a few minutes before cooking.

3. When using onions, make sure to consume them immediately after peeling and cutting as onion absorbs toxins from the atmosphere.

4. Make maximum use of food items that grow above the soil. Restrict the use of tubers like potato, carrot, and beetroot and go for vegetables that grow in sunlight.

5. If you are a fan of deep-fried foods, you can cook with less oil without compromising on the taste. For example, instead of deep-frying meat, fish, and veggies in oil, you can boil them with a little water in the pressure cooker and when all the water is absorbed, add a teaspoon of oil and sauté on a non-stick pan. You can also grill or bake them with a little oil coating on the surface.

6. If you have a very sweet tooth, substitute refined white sugar with jaggery, unrefined brown sugar, or stevia. You can also add dry fruits like dates or figs to your juices instead of sugar. Honey is another healthy substitute.

7. Sprouting legumes like green gram, cowpea, and chickpea are great for adding nutritional value to your diet.

8. Last but not the least, practice mindful eating. Be conscious of each morsel of food you take into your mouth, chew them well, and savour every flavour before swallowing. Say thank you before and after every meal.

Lesson 2: Exercise and Breathwork

Exercising is truly the most underrated healing tool. There isn't a single health problem where exercise won't benefit you. Regular exercise can slow or help prevent heart disease, stroke, high blood pressure, high cholesterol, type 2 diabetes, arthritis, osteoporosis (bone loss), etc. and reduce the risk of some cancers, including colon, breast, uterine, and lung cancer.

Apart from being beneficial for your body, exercise also improves your mental function and mood, thus reducing the risk of depression. 'Exercise produces a relaxation response that serves as a positive distraction,' says Cedric Bryant, the chief exercise physiologist at the American Council on Exercise. It stimulates your body to release proteins and other chemicals that improve the functioning of your brain by triggering a positive feeling and better mental clarity. It also helps to keep your thinking, learning, and decision-making skills sharp as you age.

Here again, there is no hard and fast rule of universal applicability. The thumb rule is to get your body moving every single day, ideally in the open air, for at least an hour. You don't have to go to a gym invariably to stay healthy. If you feel good in the gym, fantastic, but exercising in fresh air has benefits galore. While some may find walking, jogging, cycling, or swimming to be rejuvenating, others may find aerobics, Zumba, yoga, t'ai chi, qigong, or Pilates better. Find out what resonates with you and try to blend it into your daily life.

Also, try to make it fun. If you keep doing just one type of exercise, monotony may creep in. Having a combination of activities that can be divided on different days of the week is a great way to keep yourself motivated. However, make sure to stick to a schedule. I personally find traditional exercises like yoga and t'ai chi, which incorporate the mind as well as the body, more effective than just plain physical movement. Being from a country where yoga is an integral part of the cultural heritage, I can very well advocate for its holistic benefits and overall effectiveness.

The first time I enrolled for a yoga class was during the most tumultuous phase of my life—I was going through my divorce and the toll of single parenting was weighing me down—and yoga literally transformed me both physically and mentally. But after a few months of following the same routine, I found it difficult to adhere to the slow movements, concentrate on breathing, and stay still during the asanas. It was then that I understood that yoga alone would not suffice. So, I tried other options like aerobics, dancing, weight training, and cardio exercises at the gym. I found that dancing to my favourite music, either in the form of Zumba or aerobics, relaxed and uplifted my mood so much that I used to eagerly look forward to those sessions. Then, I created a regimen of mixing the two modalities on different days of a week under the guidance of a well-trained instructor.

So, you see, it is up to each one of us to identify what works well for us at every stage of life and adapt our exercise routines accordingly.

Note: Do take expert advice and evaluate your health status by a professional before embarking on any exercise schedule. Doing strenuous workouts without proper knowledge of your anatomy and physiology can do more harm than good in the long run. Also, never begin any physical activity without the guidance of a trainer. Incorrect postures and routines have been known to cause many unwanted complications.

2.2 Breathwork

Breathing is a necessity of life and it usually occurs without much thought. Though we think of breathing as an involuntary, natural process, the truth is that a majority of us do not breathe in the correct manner. Learning to breathe properly is a vital tool for wellness. Breathing affects the functioning of our body and every physiological, psychological, and emotional state results in a corresponding breathing pattern. When you breathe in air, blood cells receive oxygen and release carbon dioxide. Improper breathing can upset the oxygen and carbon dioxide exchange and contribute to panic attacks, fatigue, and other physical and emotional disturbances. For example, stressful emotions like anger, anxiety, and nervousness induce fast, short, and shallow breathing. Slowing down your breathing can directly reduce the intensity of these emotions.

Generally, there are two types of breathing patterns: diaphragmatic (abdominal) breathing and thoracic (chest) breathing. When we are under any stressful conditions like the ones mentioned above, we tend to take rapid, shallow breaths that come directly from the chest. This type of breathing is called thoracic or chest breathing. During abdominal or diaphragmatic breathing, we take even, deep breaths that come from the upper part of the abdomen. This is how we breathe when we are in a relaxed state like when we are sleeping or enjoying a good movie.

So, during stressful and anxious times, try to be aware of your breathing pattern and deliberately slow it down by taking deep breaths. You can determine your breathing pattern by placing one hand on your upper abdomen near the waist and the other on the middle part of your chest. As you breathe, notice which hand raises the most. If you are breathing properly, your abdomen should expand and contract with each breath.

During your exercise routine, incorporate a few minutes to practise diaphragmatic breathing and make it a habit. Inhale slowly and deeply through your nose. Keep your shoulders relaxed. Your abdomen should expand, while your chest should move only minimally. Exhale slowly through your mouth. As you blow air out, purse your lips slightly but keep your jaw relaxed. Repeat this breathing exercise whenever you catch yourself in a stressful situation. Do it several times until you start to feel better.

Pranayama is the formal practice of controlling the breath. This mindful breathing exercise, which has many variations under different names, can be mastered under the guidance of a trained instructor within a matter of a few days. Once you learn to incorporate it into your exercise routine, with the backup of a self-affirming phrase or mantra, your mind opens to new channels of clarity, peace, and total well-being.

Lesson 3: Relaxation and Recreation

The word relax comes from the Latin words *re* and *lax*, which means 'to be less tense and anxious.' When translated in physiological terms, it means to loosen up, take rest, and engage in some enjoyable activity that makes you less rigid and helps you 're-create' yourself (recreation).

Relaxation and recreation are extremely important amidst the busyness of life. Catering to the needs of children, juggling time and energy between home and career, and all the stress and strain that goes with it will tear you into bits and pieces. If you don't find ways to relax, I guarantee you that in the long run, you will be eating medicines as food and lamenting about the dismal destiny you have been bestowed with.

When it comes to parenting, having the company of a partner allows for moments when you can slip away, confer with another grown-up, or receive an assuring hug or relaxing sex when life feels overwhelming. But single moms have to jam so much into a 24-hour day that often they are left with no time to breathe, let alone fully relax. That is why it is extremely important to find some 'me time' once in a while.

You cannot make excuses and blame your children or circumstances for lack of time. Do your children demand that you cater to only their needs and deny all your own pleasures? Do they ask all your time to be spent with them? No, they do not. Whatever lifestyle you adopt is exclusively your choice. Children invariably adapt to any circumstance you put them through. So, it is ultimately your choice to decide how you will spend your days. Taking out time to relax, rejuvenate, and recreate yourself is the greatest gift you can give yourself and your children in the long run. Children outgrow their need to be under your wings and fly out of the nest and then you are left with a vacuum. Empty nest syndrome triggers a whole lot of problems if you don't know the ways to take care of yourself. A healthy old age without having to be a burden to your grown-up children is the ultimate gift of love you can give them.

Relaxation can occur on a daily basis and in packages. Your daily relaxation habits can be started with a good one to two hours of exclusive time with yourself, which you can break into short modules across the day, followed by seven to eight hours of uninterrupted sleep. Ideally, try to start your day before sunrise, with a short prayer of gratitude and rituals that will connect you to the energy of the universe. You can spend the next hour doing any morning activity that you like—gratitude journaling, exercising, listening to relaxing music, or dancing. Also, try to find instances throughout the day when you can go into yourself, stretch your body, and tune into acts you enjoy, like going out for a walk, watching films, cooking, painting, or any other hobby which makes you happy.

Set goals and reward achievements with indulgences. Spoil yourself, whether that means enjoying your favourite food or binge-watching your favourite show. Find something you love to do and do it often. Treat yourself with love and affection.

Find ways to support yourself. Find friends of the same wavelength. Socialise and have fun. There is a lot of research on loneliness, and all of it shows the horrifying consequences of being lonely. Loneliness won't just make you miserable; it will kill you. Chronic loneliness increases your likelihood of early death by fourteen per cent says a study. Loneliness causes high blood pressure and high cholesterol. It even suppresses the functioning of your immune system, making you vulnerable to all kinds of illnesses and diseases. In fact, scientists have concluded that chronic loneliness poses as significant a risk for your long-term health and longevity as cigarette smoking. So, do reach out to friends and allow them to help you. Remember it takes a strong person to ask for help when one needs it. Also, go on trips and outings with friends. Plan holidays and explore nature. Step outside, breathe, and appreciate who you are. It has been proven that natural landscapes accelerate recovery from stress. Take a hike in the mountains or go for a walk on the beach. All these are highly beneficial as nature can create positive changes in the brain. More importantly, it's easy to love yourself in the relaxed rhythm of the natural world.

Have fun with everything you do. Let yourself express the joy of living. When you smile, laugh, and rejoice, the universe rejoices with you! Take life easily, playfully, lovingly, non-seriously. 'Seriousness is a disease, the greatest disease of the soul and playfulness the greatest health,' said Osho, the great mystic.

3.2 Sleep

Adequate sleep (at least seven-eight hours) is needed every single day to relax and rejuvenate your body and mind. Do not overlook the benefits of good sleep and if ever you have an issue of insomnia, find ways to overcome it.

I encourage and insist that my clients develop a disciplined routine of going to bed and waking up at a fixed time every day. Spend the last few minutes before bed with gratitude, affirmations for the next day, or listening to soothing music. Wear the most comfortable and tidy clothes and use aromas to soothe your nerves. A good perfume or any aromatic essential oils or creams will do magic for your nerves. The lighting and comfort of the room and bed are also very important. Decorate the walls and shelves with positive soothing artefacts and never ever allow a gadget into your bed like a smartphone or laptop. Reading a book is also a good way to end the day, and if it is a spiritual or motivational book, then even better. Also, listen to your biological clock and go to bed before 10:30 p.m. and wake up before sunrise.

Lesson 4: Sex and Relationships

No saga of a woman's life, and for that matter, anybody born human, is complete without delving into the sexual orientation and needs unique to each of them. Though a topic that is still considered taboo in many cultures around the world, it is one of the most basic human instincts and the underlying cause of a whole lot of issues, especially when it comes to this particular community of single moms.

It is a relief that the New Age world is inclusive of all types of sexual orientations, including the LGBTQ community, and open to discussions about masturbation and other forms of sex. It is a welcome change that broadens the mindset of the world regarding sexuality.

The sexual need of every individual is unique to her/him and addressing it is by no means an offence or sin. Being separated from a spouse or being a full-time mom never implies that she has lost all her biological urges and is exiled to lead a life of celibacy. Nature didn't put those organs and hormones into her solely for the purpose of reproduction, and though that definitely is an important purpose, they are there also to provide her pleasure and relaxation.

The benefits of a good sexual routine cannot be nullified or dismissed by any means of logic. There may be a very small per cent of highly evolved beings who have acquired the skill to convert their sexual energies to higher frequencies through spiritual practices of kundalini tantra or meditation, but it is not everyone's cup of tea, at least not for a single mom already struggling to stay afloat in a life full of challenges. The majority of single moms I have met carry the baggage of painful sexual experiences. Some of them do not even know what a beautiful orgasm is even though they may have given birth to more than one child.

As part of my protocol as a healer, I need to get the sexual history of every client, and usually, they don't hesitate or feel inhibited because, by the time we reach that part of their personality, we would have already built the rapport and trust needed in such a relationship. I find that many of my clients come with diseases of the sexual organs due to constant suppression both when they were with a partner and after that. They have either been sexually insulted or abused or were just dissatisfied with their partners in bed. In the case of widows, they were forced into self-imposed celibacy. These suppressions invariably upset the balance of their bodies and minds as you can see in the stories I have presented. Most of them had problems with their uterus, ovaries, or breast and, of course, thyroid, which is the organ that controls the metabolism of the body. So, it is high time that this hushed up part of a single mother's life is addressed and discussed openly. Indian women are still far behind their Western counterparts in addressing their needs, though the new generation of single moms, who are mostly in their twenties or thirties, is better at voicing their needs and even date openly.

Many of these women find outlets in secret relationships with colleagues, bosses, or friends but never ever feel secure about it themselves. These partners are mostly married men who have to keep up their image in society and seldom acknowledge their relationship openly. A few bold women cohabitate with their boyfriends, but this forms a very small percentage in the so-called rich cultural setup of modern India. Most of them are just reconciled to the fact that they can no longer have an active sexual life and do not find the courage to give marriage a second try, the reasons being varied and complex.

So, what is the importance of this sexual stimulation? Why is it so necessary to have an orgasm once in a while? Sex, like any other metabolic activity, be it urination, defecation, or breathing, is a natural instinct, the balance and harmony of which is necessary to sustain the body and mind in optimum health. Some of the upsides of a good sex life, collated from various research studies I have come across, have been summed up below.

1. 'Sexually active people take fewer sick days,' says Yvonne K. Fulbright, Ph.D, a sexual health expert. Good sexual life keeps the immune system humming which defends the body against germs, viruses, and other intruders. Yvonne further elaborates that for women, regular sex increases vaginal lubrication, blood flow, and elasticity, all of which make sex feel better and help you crave more of it. It also improves women's bladder control. Good sex is like a workout for your pelvic floor muscles. When you have an orgasm, it causes contractions in those muscles, which strengthens them.

2. 'Research suggests a link between sex and lower blood pressure,' says Joseph J. Pinzone, MD, CEO and,

medical director of Amai Wellness. 'One landmark study found that sexual intercourse lowered systolic blood pressure. It bumps up your heart rate and uses various muscles, thereby lowering heart attack risk. Sex helps keep your estrogen and testosterone levels in balance,' Pinzone adds.

3.   'Sex lessens pain,' says Barry R. Komisaruk, Ph.D and a distinguished service professor at Rutgers, the State University of New Jersey. 'Before you reach for an aspirin, try for an orgasm. Orgasm can block pain. It releases a hormone that helps raise your pain threshold. Vaginal stimulation can block chronic back and leg pain, and many women have told that genital self-stimulation can reduce menstrual cramps, arthritic pain, and in some cases, even headache.'

4.   Sex improves sleep. 'After orgasm, the hormone prolactin is released, which is responsible for the feelings of relaxation and sleepiness after sex,' says Sheenie Ambardar, MD. She is a psychiatrist in West Hollywood, California.

5.   Sex eases stress as being close to your partner can soothe stress and anxiety. Touching and hugging can release your body's natural 'feel-good hormone'.

From the above data, it is obvious that a good sexual life is imperative for a fully relaxed body and mind. If you choose to be celibate and your body is okay with it, do so by all means. But if your body calls for sexual intimacy and orgasmic release, never ever hesitate to address your needs in a safe environment. While masturbation is a choice endorsed by many of the women I have interviewed, it does not produce as much oxytocin and other happy hormones as a healthy, emotional, and loving intercourse with a partner does. For many single moms, the additional burden of a committed relationship deters them from reaching out to men and thus they resort to masturbation. There are women I have encountered who went for a lesbian relationship after their frustrating experiences with men and found it more soothing and safer, since they felt that women understood each other better, both emotionally and physically.

So, as a healer, I cannot advise one form of sexual stimulation just as I cannot advocate one form of exercise or diet universally for everyone. These are purely personal choices and it is up to you to decide what resonates with your comfort level, culture, and needs. I only exhort you to stop suppressing your personal needs from the fear of disapproval or the wrath of people around you. It is also important to be very open about your relationships with your children and to discuss your needs with them. Usually, the new generation of youngsters are much more liberated and they will understand and honour your choices.

Once, my twenty-four-year-old son asked me, 'Momma, why don't you ever go for a holiday to resorts as everybody does? I have never seen you going on trips without me.'

I said, 'Son, mostly it is couples who go out on such holidays. It is not safe for solo women to go to remote places for holidays in our country.'

I was really amused by his answer. 'Okay, then find a boyfriend, go out with him, have your own gala time, momma. I can even suggest you dating sites for single parents. It is a whole big community out there.'

I have included this hilarious conversation here to enlighten you that your children can become your greatest allies in every area of your life once you take them into confidence.

Before concluding the topic, I reiterate: never hesitate to build a good sex life as per your comfort, either in wedlock or out of it. The world has changed so much and has become inclusive of every style of life that you can opt for. In short, be unapologetically you.

Lesson 5: Spirituality and Meditation

5.1 Spirituality

The word spirituality holds different meanings for different people. While religion and spirituality are commonly considered to be closely related, if not synonymous, Webb (2007) proposes a model wherein the term spirituality is redefined to be more accurately employed as a single construct with three inter-related dimensions:

1. Religious spirituality (RS): A structured connection with deity.
2. Theistic spirituality (TS): A non-structured connection with deity.
3. Existential spirituality (ES): A non-theistic search for meaning and purpose.

Let's examine the meaning of this much talked about yet very abstract term. I will begin with my story. Though I am a Muslim by birth, my parents, who were inclusive and tolerant towards all religions, fed me with the notion that spirituality is all about unconditional acceptance and love between all organisms on earth. Yet I was confused and terrified about the abstract concepts of hell and heaven which were injected into my little mind by the local priests of our customary Quran classes. I could not connect with the verses of the Holy Quran where God is depicted as someone up there watching your every action and punishing you for your sins. Thus started my relentless search for God and the true meaning of spirituality.

After years of exploring every religious scripture and metaphysical concept, I finally embarked upon a very interesting book called *E-Squared* by Pam Grout which literally struck me like a thunderbolt of realisation about the existence of that universal energy in the most humorous yet scientific way. She has structured the book like a set of scientific experiments which you can do on your own and actually perceive the presence of that reservoir of energy. Doing the nine experiments with Pam Grout felt like a homecoming. All the tidbits of information acquired through my search fell into place. I then read the scriptures once again from a whole new light and everything made sense.

I understood that every ritual, religion, and metaphysical philosophy finally culminates in that one universal truth. All the doctrines in them have been designed to discipline and channelise the human mind. If carried out with belief, they take you to the same destination. It is the propagators of religions with vested interests that create an avalanche of confusion by misinterpreting the scriptures and misguiding many an innocent seeker of truth. Thus, the construct of existential spirituality, which implies searching for one's higher purpose and meaning of life, became appealing to me rather than adhering to a specific structured pattern of conducting one's life according to a set of rules laid down by priesthood.

I then began to believe in one omnipresent energy that permeates the entire cosmos of which we all are an integral part. We are born with a speck of this energy called life force in our bodies which sustains us till death after which it returns to its original source. All our life experiences depend on the vibrating frequencies of this energy. When we vibrate at the higher frequencies of love, compassion, and peace, they become our life realities. When we vibrate at lower frequencies of fear, hate, resentment, and sadness, these aspects become our realities. Hence, to me, God is just the personification of the three attributes of the universe:

- G: Generator
- O: Operator
- D: Destroyer

This completes the cycle of every perceivable object on earth.

I don't believe in a God who is sitting up there punishing you for your sins and rewarding you for virtues. Rather, I believe that this power called God resides in each of us as reservoirs of love, wisdom, and guidance. This is also connotated by the term *Aham Brahmasmi,* which means 'I am Brahma (the creator)'. If we are vigilant enough to listen to it and take guidance from it, we will have answers to every baffling question in life. However, my ideology of non-theistic spirituality doesn't make the notions of religious spirituality or theistic spirituality wrong. They are all different ways of perceiving the same universal truth.

Teachers and guides have manifested at all times to guide us to this ultimate truth, in the form of prophets, enlightened humans, written literature, and metaphysical intuitive experiences. This power/spirit gives glimpses of its existence through a myriad of life experiences, both painful and joyous. In all our stories, we have seen a moment of realisation engulfing each of the protagonists at some point, after which they are motivated to find their authentic self. In Gauri's case, it was a message on the phone and her guru, Paramahansa Yogananda, that led her to seek her healing. In Reetha's case, it was her yoga guru and reiki master. For Ayesha, it was the activity of gratitude journaling, while for Maria, the answer came in the form of an astrologer.

Thus, you see that we are given experiences that literally pull us out of our comfort zones, break us, and destroy us until we hit rock bottom and that's when an epiphany occurs which puts all our experiences, good or bad, into perspective. We get a glimpse of the existence of the universal power far beyond our levels of comprehension. From that moment onwards, we get connected to it and experience that sense of fulfilment and peace from which nothing and nobody can disturb us. We get initiated into our ultimate calling and purpose in life.

It is not necessary that we hit rock bottom to attain spiritual awakening. We can access it even without suffering, just by practising a few rituals on a regular basis throughout life. Rituals are nothing but a set of practices that connect us to a particular outcome through deep focus and intention. Rituals have been created from time immemorial for every occasion. Be it a holy mass communion, a marriage ceremony, a graduation ceremony, a thanksgiving dinner, or a temple pooja, you get to see a set of practices that signifies the event. Haven't you seen rituals to mark the beginning of a day in companies or of duty hand over in army camps and hospitals? They are all just practices to anchor the intention and attention of all involved to the immediate task and to connect with each other at an energetic level. So, rituals are all about focus and connection. While doing rituals, the mind gets focused with no distractions. All your sense organs are channelised to focus on the intention of the ritual. This creates high-frequency energy vibrations conducive to the occasion.

When it comes to spirituality, rituals aid in accessing the higher centres of existence by connecting and integrating the mind, body, and soul. Let me explain this with an example. Imagine a holy mass ceremony in a church. Your eyes are focused on the artefacts at the altar and the priest, your ears are focused on the serene music from the church choir and the discourse from the priest, your nostrils inhale the soothing fragrances of incense, you taste the symbolic wine and bread with your tongue, and your hands are either clasped together or clapping. You are requested to move your body into kneeling and standing positions at intervals. Thus, all your sense organs are stimulated and channelised to the atmosphere of the chapel. Your thoughts and emotions are focused and you become intensely aware of your immediate surroundings. Your sense of perception increases and you feel grounded and calm. In this heightened state of awareness, you get answers to your prayers and have intuitive and healing experiences. The same happens in temples, mosques, monasteries, and other spiritual gatherings. It also happens with individuals who know how to harness their inner power through rituals.

Rituals need not be religious to become effective. The shifts of energy occur due to collective intention towards the desired outcome and not necessarily due to religious beliefs. They act as catalysts to uncover your inherent capabilities and powers inside you. They take you to the heart of your problems and to their solutions.

You can create your own set of rituals to connect to yourself and the universal power. Create a sacred space for yourself at any corner or room of your house. Set up an altar where you can always turn to when in need of rejuvenation or guidance. Decorate it with images and artefacts that resonate with your spiritual orientation. Books, quotes, candles, lamps, incense sticks, essential oils, water, crystals, bells, and dongs are just some of the objects that aid in creating a conducive atmosphere. If you will closely observe, the use of fragrances, light, sound, eatables/water, and physical gestures are an integral part of every ritual. You can do your prayers (if you are a believer), meditation, reading, chanting, breathwork, journaling, or even simply sit quietly and ask for guidance from the universe. All you need is to feel calm, alert, and serene in your self-created space. You get answers, you get insights, you feel peaceful and tranquil whenever you enter the area with intention.

I have my own set of rituals and practices and an altar that does not conform to any structured religion. The first thing I do after stepping out of the bedroom in the morning is light candles and incense sticks at my altar. I sit there for a while, staring and blinking at the flame for a few minutes while breathing slowly to relax my whole body. Then I do whatever practice I have set an intention on that day. I chant from any of the spiritual books (Quran, Gita, or Bible) or read any self-help or motivational book. I then do my namaz or my energy healing modules of eutaptics or chakra cleansing. I follow it up with my affirmations and journaling. Whenever I embark upon a new healing tool like gratitude or mirror work, I always make it a point to practise it sitting there. In the end, I say a closing prayer like *aum shanti*, amen, peace, or *alhamdulillah*. I try to revisit the space at sunset if I am home and before going to bed. Any time I need an answer or solution for a situation, I just get into the energy of the space, sit quietly with my eyes shut, and listen to my inner self. I can say from repeated experiences that it works every time. Answers can come in the form of flashes of words or images or just as intuitive thoughts. Sometimes, I get the answer for the intention set at the altar later in the day or in a dream but it always comes.

The universe is abundant with possibilities and ready to manifest in front of the seeker. 'He that seeketh findeth; and to him that knocketh it shall be opened.' This biblical phrase stands true to this moment. (The power and necessity of rituals have been extensively dealt with in the book *Your Hidden Riches* by Janet and Chris Attwood)

5.2 Meditation

Meditation is a technique to train your mind and increase awareness just as physical exercise is an approach to train the body. It quietens the mind and allows you to access the highly creative and intuitive dimensions of life. Meditation helps you uncover your subconscious thought patterns. It allows you to categorise them into what is wholesome or negative. It resets the structure and functioning of your brain when done in the right way. This is the best time to rewire your subconscious mind and change whatever negative thought patterns you have to positive ones. When your mind is quietened by meditation, the best ideas flow and that is when you can make the best decisions. Your spiritual connection also increases with meditation.

In 2011, Sara Lazar and her team at Harvard found out that mindfulness meditation can actually change the structure of the brain. During the eight weeks of mindfulness-based stress reduction (MBSR), they noticed an increase in the cortical thickness of the hippocampus (part of the brain that governs learning and memory) and in certain other areas of the brain which play an important role in emotion regulation and self-referential processing. There were also decreases in brain cell volume in the amygdala, which is responsible for fear, anxiety, and stress. These changes matched the participants' self-reports of their stress levels, indicating that meditation not only changes the brain but also changes our subjective perception and feelings as well.

How to Meditate

There are various meditation techniques: mantra meditation, spiritual meditation, focused meditation, visualisation meditation, chakra meditation, vipassana meditation, transcendental meditation, and walking meditation, to name a few. You can try any of them and find out what resonates with you.

The simplest form of meditation consists of the following steps:

- Sit or lie comfortably.
- Close your eyes.
- Make no effort to control the breath; simply breathe naturally.
- Focus your attention on the breath and on how the body moves with each inhalation and exhalation.
- Notice the movement of your body as you breathe.
- If your mind wanders, return your focus back to your breath.
- Observe your chest, shoulders, rib cage, and belly.

Do this meditation practice for two to three minutes in the beginning, and then try it for longer periods.

Meditation can also be done by repeating a single word or mantra, staring at a candle flame, listening to a repetitive gong, or counting beads on a rosary. Meditative practices in the East always include the chanting of any mantra or phrase like 'aum' or 'amen' or 'so hum', which helps you to get focused and get in touch with your higher centres. Dr Wayne W. Dyer advocates using the phrase 'I Am' during meditation and completing it with whatever changes or results you want in your life. For example, 'I am strong', 'I am loved', etc. These are called affirmative phrases. In this form of meditation, you simply refocus your awareness on the chosen object of attention each time you notice your mind wandering. Rather than pursuing random thoughts, you simply let them go. With practice, an inner balance develops. Meditation can be incorporated into your morning ritual or at any time of the day when you have a few minutes of uninterrupted silence.

Lesson 6: Taming the Subconscious

i.   Affirmations and Visualisations

What are affirmations? Put simply, whatever you say or think is an affirmation. Any statement that you make to yourself, either positive or negative, is an affirmation. We think about 80,000 thoughts per day and almost eighty per cent of them are repetitive. These thoughts affect each and every one of our experiences in life. 'We are what we think. With our thoughts, we make our world.' The Buddha spoke these insightful words over 2,500 years ago.

As we know, our mind functions through two parts—the conscious and the subconscious. Science says that ninety per cent of our mind is made up of the subconscious part and just ten per cent represents our conscious part. Our belief systems are formed by the thoughts we are subconsciously trained to think from our childhood and the words we speak to ourselves throughout the day. The subconscious mind has no filtering system and does not know false from true or negative from positive. It accepts all that we say and think and utilises them as the material to build our life scripts.

Affirmations act as messages to our subconscious and establish habitual ways of thinking and behaving. When we learn to create and repeat affirmations that are positive, through conscious effort, we will be planting new seeds in the fertile soil of our subconscious mind. They create new beliefs for our consciousness to respond to and make them true. Thus, positive affirmations act as a powerful tool to help us change our mood, state of mind, and manifest the change we desire in our life. They can be used to change any area of our life: health, career, and relationships. They plant healing thoughts and ideas that support us in developing self-confidence and self-esteem and creating peace of mind and inner joy. In short, by repeating positive affirmations, we are setting an 'inner compass' that will gradually shift our behaviour permanently.

But affirmations work best if we can first identify the unwholesome or negative beliefs from positive ones. For example, many of us can remember being told as a child by a teacher, parent, or relative that we didn't have the ability to do something or that we are a failure. These negative statements can stay with us in the subconscious mind which we then reinforce throughout our lives. When we become aware of those negative beliefs, we can create statements that are the exact opposite of them. For example, 'I am capable', 'I am a winner', or 'I believe in my capabilities'. As we reprogram our mind with such positive statements, we move from the concept of the affirmation to a real and positive embodiment of the quality we seek.

We have seen the effects of subconscious patterns in some of our stories. We saw how Simran had the fear of abandonment and poverty consciousness from her childhood experiences which reflected throughout her adult life. We saw how Gauri and Sara attracted the replicas of their fathers as their partners due to their belief that men are not emotionally available. We have also seen how Maria created a whole new reality by changing her childhood script with affirmations. So, you see, we all have it in us to create a reality of our choosing through our thoughts and words. We have the power to change any negative situation in life by repeating positive affirmations. However, like any new skill, affirmations must be practised until they become second nature.

How to Use Affirmations Effectively

Make a list of what you have always thought of as your negative qualities. Include all criticisms others have made about you that you have been holding onto. It can be something your siblings, parents, or peers used to say about you when you were a child. When you write out each of those recurring beliefs, notice if you are holding on to it anywhere in your body. For example, do you feel tightness or dread in your heart or stomach when you think about a particular criticism or negative belief?

Now write an affirmation that is the opposite of that belief and embodies the positive change you would like to see in yourself. Do note that affirmations should always be written in the first person, in present tense or present continuous tense and every word in it should be positive. For example, if you want to change your belief that you are a failure, your affirmation should be 'I am a winner'. You don't say 'I am not a failure' or use any negative words. If you want a pain to disappear, you don't say 'I am pain free'. Instead, you say 'I am getting healed' or 'I am perfectly healthy'. You don't use the word pain at all because that is the negative reality you want to change.

Write out the affirmation several times in a notebook and speak them out loud. Then anchor the positive affirmation in your body as you are repeating it by placing your hand on the area that felt uncomfortable when you wrote out the negative belief. Also, breathe in the affirmation while you are saying or writing it. If doubts, fears, or negative thoughts come up, just recognise them for what they are: old limiting beliefs that want to stay around. They have no power over you. Tell them gently, 'Out! I no longer need you.' Then replace them with positive affirmations.

However, the mechanical repetition of words isn't enough to create change. To really make affirmations work, you need to charge it with a lot of emotion. Emotions create the energy shift to embody the affirmation as they are really energy set in motion (e-motion). You need to feel the energy of the new reality you want to manifest and actually see it in your mind's eye as if it is already happening. This is called visualisation.

Visualisation consists of imagining, seeing, or describing something you would like to create. 'Visualisations create an inner landscape that in turn produces results on the outside,' says Dr Patricia J Crane in her book *Ordering from the Cosmic Kitchen*. 'It gets you into the relaxed state with alpha brain waves for rehearsing the inner changes that become the outer reality.'

While affirmation is auditory and verbal, visualisation is visual and non-verbal. When used together, they speed up the process of change you wish to bring about in your life. Add to it a lot of feeling and the process is accelerated even further. The feeling part (emotion) while you visualise your desired outcome actually creates the energy shift to make it true. The universe responds to the feelings that you send out more than the mechanical repetition of words.

How to Use Visualisations Effectively

First, decide exactly what is it that you want to create. Second, create a mental picture of what you desire. Use powerful images that embody your goal, such as seeing yourself holding an award or living in your dream house. Feel the emotions of happiness and excitement while seeing the image. Third, focus lightly on this picture and feeling, during your meditation routine as well as during the day. Use positive affirmations to give your goal additional energy.

Affirmations and visualisations when done with total belief and feeling can thus neutralise the past and create the future you desire. When it comes to healing your body, it is best to stand in front of the mirror and repeat each new thought pattern several times. You can also write them down. Then, if there is any part of your body you still dislike or have a problem with, use that particular affirmation daily until the positive change takes place. Give this part extra attention so you may go beyond the limitation. Your body will start responding by healing your problem and giving excellent health by functioning as a harmonious whole. For example, if you have a pain in your knees, place your hands on your knee and say 'My knee is getting healed' and 'I am able to run freely' and actually visualise and feel the ease of running with a pain-free knee. Soon you will have a body you really love. You will even find your weight normalising, posture straightening, and skin glowing.

Now that you know the power of words, avoid all negative self-talk. Because single parents don't have a partner to cheer them through the tough parenting moments, negative talk can be particularly challenging to avoid. Kids often push us to our limits and accentuate our feelings of inadequacy. Catch yourself whenever you go down that lane of negativity and transmute them to positive affirmations.

Here are some sample affirmations you can use to improve any area of your life from Dr Patricia. J. Crane and Rick Nichols, who are the torch bearers of Louise L. Hay's teachings (www.heartinspired.com).

- I love and accept myself exactly as I am right here and right now.
- My body is strong and vibrantly healthy.
- My income is constantly increasing, and I deserve it!
- My relationships are harmonious.
- I am guided by divine wisdom for all my decisions.
- I enjoy a wonderful career with meaning and purpose.

For more on affirmations and visualisations, visit: www.healyourlifetraining.com/blog. Also, read *Creative Visualizations* by Shakti Gawain and *Ordering from the Cosmic Kitchen* by Dr Patricia J. Crane (Ph.D).

ii. Mirror Work

Mirror work or mirror play is another tool to reinforce the power of affirmations. It is one of the most profound tools to learn to love and accept yourself and thereby create a foundation for real love and abundance to manifest in every area of your life.

As mentioned several times before, love is the greatest healing power. It can heal even the deepest and most painful memories because love brings the light of understanding to the dark corners of our minds. Mirror work utilises this power of love. It consists of appreciating yourself and your being in front of a mirror. The more you use mirrors for complimenting yourself, accepting yourself, and supporting yourself, the deeper and more enjoyable your relationship with yourself will become. This is because the mirror reflects back to you the feelings you have about yourself. It makes you immediately aware of where you are resisting and where you are open and flowing. It clearly shows you what thoughts you will need to change in order to accept yourself completely.

As you learn to do mirror work, you will become much more aware of the words you say to yourself and how you treat yourself. This way, you will learn to take care of yourself on a deeper level and become less self-critical, and very soon, your mirror will become your companion and a dear friend. As you continue to do your mirror work, you will also develop new and healthy habits of the mind that will open the door to a joyous and fulfilling life.

How to Do Mirror Work

You can add mirror work to your morning ritual. For example, before you brush your teeth, look into your eyes and say the following to your reflection in the bathroom mirror:

- I love and approve of myself exactly as I am.
- I am safe.
- I am willing to change.

My mentor, Dr G. L. Sampoorna, says that there is nothing that is impossible once you impregnate your mind with these three affirmations throughout your life. You can say other affirmations as well which you relate to. The only point to remember here is that they need to be said with conviction and feeling. You can also use mirror work to forgive yourself and others and release negative emotions and feelings you are holding on to. Keep a small mirror handy in your bag and use it often.

iii. Gratitude Journaling

We have discussed and understood the benefits of gratitude journaling in the first chapter. We have seen how the positive energy associated with gratitude activates the brain (the reticular activating system) and creates a filter through which we are enabled to envision a life of immense possibilities and invariably attract them. The happy hormones—the endorphins, serotonin, and dopamine—get activated by our act of saying 'thank you' with feeling and visualising the outcomes. Gratitude is just another form of affirmation and self-hypnosis/autosuggestion.

How to Practise Gratitude Journaling

1. Whenever possible, deliberately think and say 'thank you' with absolute feeling. Keep a journal where you can write about everything you feel grateful for. The more gratitude you give out, the more abundance there will be. Gratitude must become a way of life and it should impregnate your cells and subconscious mind.

2. All you need to do is maintain a list of your dreams and aspirations in every area of life and say thank you for each of them. You can categorise them as follows:

- Health and body
- Career/work
- Money
- Relationships
- Personal desires
- Material things

3. This is how Rhonda Byrne has arranged her book, *The Magic*. Out of the twenty-eight days of gratitude practice, the first twelve days are for gratitude for what you have now and had in the past. The next ten days are for desires and dreams you want to manifest. The last six days are for the higher levels of existence.

4. Initially, you can follow the twenty-eight-day practice in consequence. Later on, you can choose one area that requires a change and practise gratitude for that specific area for three or more days in a row.

As I said earlier, when I practised this life-changing module for twenty-eight days in a row, I was completely transformed. All my life situations magically changed for the better and I started propagating the message through my seminars, workshops, and patients. I learnt to find something to be grateful for in every situation of life and change whatever was not in my interest with the same tool.

iv. Inner Child Analysis

The topic of inner child analysis is becoming very popular in all modalities of psychological healing and there is a lot of research and literature on the topic. The book *Homecoming* by John Bradshaw is an insightful and authentic study on the subject. Another significant work on inner child analysis can be found in the healing module of Louise L. Hay, which is by far the simplest form of exercise I have witnessed and has far-reaching benefits for the practitioner.

The crux of inner child analysis is that we all have a little child in us which is the echo of what we are today. Working with the inner child helps to heal the traumas of the past. To truly redeem ourselves from our past, we need to revisit the experiences of the child we once were and find out what our own script says about our life and the unfolding drama we have been recreating and repeating in our lives. For example, if you had a very dominating and narcissistic father who oppressed your mother who, in turn, played the role of a victim, you grow up with the image that women are victims and should be submissive to every nuance of their husbands. Though your logical mind learns that it is not right, you tend to attract a partner very similar to your father. This was seen in Gauri's and Simran's stories.

Again, if your parents or immediate caretakers, like nannies or grannies, were extremely strict or angry all the time, you develop the fear of punishment and lack of confidence, whilst if they feed you with inputs of encouragement and positivity, you tend to become confident and be at ease in every situation. Similarly, if you were always insulted or ridiculed in front of others, either about your looks or your capabilities, you grow up with a sense of lack and inadequacy, self-hatred, and inferiority complex. Whereas, if you were brought up with a lot of appreciation, you grow up with great self-esteem and love.

So, what can we do to help our inner child? For this, we need to learn how to meet, rescue, and adopt this wounded little soul that still lives deep inside us. We need to communicate with our inner child and let it know that we accept every single part of ourselves unconditionally. We need to learn to accept even the scared, foolish, ugly, and awkward sides we condemn and criticise ourselves for. Rescuing and reparenting our inner child will enable us to live a more positive and rewarding life filled with fun, laughter, spontaneity, authenticity, and most importantly, with love.

Inner Child Meditation Technique

If you have a photograph of yourself as a small child, it will help you to empathically reconnect with it. Just keep it in front of you while doing the exercise.

Sit comfortably and take three deep breaths. Relax every part of your body from head to toe with each breath cycle. Notice any areas of your body that are tight and consciously relax them. Now look inside yourself and find that little version of yourself who has willingly carried your traumas, who holds your memories of being abused, ignored, betrayed, abandoned, unaccepted, or unloved.

Notice how the little girl looks and feels. Comfort her, apologise to your little one for having neglected her for so long. Promise her that from now on, you will always be there for her, you will never leave her alone. Tell your child how much you love and treasure her. Praise her for all her good qualities. Tell her how special and wonderful she is. Tell her that she has nothing to feel guilty or ashamed about. None of what happened to her was ever her fault. Things will be okay and you will never let any more harm come to her.

Assure her that you will do your best to bring to her the joy that has been missing from her life. When you speak to your inner child, have a loving and soothing inner voice, one that is supportive, soft, nurturing, patient, and comforting.

Now see your child relaxed, safe, peaceful, and happy. See her laughing, playing with friends, or doing whatever you enjoyed doing in your childhood. Imagine sitting beside that little girl, putting your arm around her shoulders, and gently pulling her close.

Now see yourself playing with this child. Imagine the activities that brought joy to you as a child. It can be anything from eating an ice cream or jumping in a muddy pool during the rains. Feel the joy and innocent excitement of the moments.

Now visualise the teenager within you as she moves through the bewildering time of puberty that marks the transition from childhood to adulthood. Repeat the entire process with this teenage girl as well. Now visualise the adult in you now with love and congratulate yourself for having come this far. Tell her that she has done her best at every point in time and space.

Cherish and embrace each of those images of your inner child. Forgive those parts which no longer serve you and move on. Allow yourself to release your inner child now. Be firm and release all those limiting patterns from her to celebrate your present and future. Understand that all those experiences have enriched you in a myriad of ways and made you the magnificent person you are now, but now it is time to let go. Release that wounded child once and for all from your consciousness.

Being without your wounded inner child will feel strange for a while because you are so much used to it, but you will eventually begin to notice positive changes. You will feel lighter, less burdened, and more present in the moment. You will feel more energetic, grounded, and at peace with yourself. You may no longer complain or share your problems with close friends as you no longer give your wounds the power to pull you down.

This entire process will change you not only at a conscious level but at the subconscious level as well. Your previous perspective of how you should be and what you should do in order to be accepted by your families and society will go through a radical change. After releasing the inner child, you will no longer fit into the image of a poor, battered dependent single mom. You will become the master of your life and start celebrating your sojourn on this earth every living minute of your life.

Note: Inner child analysis yields the best results when done with a facilitator. If you are doing it alone, be prepared for some emotional reactions that can surface.

v. Forgiveness

When we cannot fully enjoy the present moment, it means that we are holding on to some negative emotions from our past. It can be regret, sadness, hurt, fear, guilt, blame, anger, resentment, or sometimes even the desire for revenge on someone you feel wronged you. Each one of these states comes from a space of unforgiveness, a refusal to let go and come back to the present moment. This only depletes and drains us as we keep running the same story over and over in our own minds to no avail. But it is foolish to punish ourselves in the present because someone hurt us in the past. This is where forgiveness comes in. Forgiveness means giving up one's hurtful feelings and just letting the whole thing go.

You just have to be willing to forgive, even if you don't know how to. You can start with forgiving yourself for anything that you feel guilty about from your past. Forgive yourself for those imperfect moments and move forward. Refuse to criticise yourself. Stop trying to compensate for being a single parent by trying to be perfect at all times. Be patient with yourself. Treat yourself as you would treat someone you really love. Love is the key to healing and the pathway to love is forgiveness. Then forgive everyone you presume to have caused you suffering, even your abusive partner who abandoned you to face all the challenges of life alone. Forgive every other person be it your family members, in-laws, or friends who you feel did injustice to you. Forgiveness is one of the greatest tools for self-healing.

Forgiveness Exercise

1. Close your eyes and sit quietly and peacefully. Think of the people in your life who are the hardest to forgive. What would you really like to do to them? What do they need to do to get your forgiveness? Imagine that happening now. Get into the details. How long do you want them to suffer or do penance?

2. Again, sit quietly with your eyes closed and say, 'The person I need to forgive is ___________ and I forgive you for ___________.' Do this over and

over. Then imagine the person you are forgiving saying thank you to you. Do this for at least five or ten minutes. Search deep in your heart for the injustices you still carry. Then let them go.

3. When you have cleared as much as you can, for now, turn your attention towards yourself. Say out loud to yourself, 'I forgive myself for ____________.' Do this for another five minutes or so. These are powerful exercises and highly effective when done at least once or twice a month. Remember that some experiences will be easier to let go, while some will have to be chipped away constantly until they dissolve. (Adapted from the Heal Your Life® modules by Louise L. Hay)

vi. Emotion Processing

Anger/resentment, fear, sadness, and guilt are the basic emotions that form the foundation of every negative situation in life. These emotions are the direct opposite of the all-consuming universal emotion of love which enfolds the varying hues of peace, joy, bliss and salvation. Experiencing each of these states is inevitable in our journey as social beings in this world. While interacting with anyone in life, including yourself, constant inner work to balance your negative emotions and to feel loved is just as important as breath is needed to sustain life.

Fear is the basic emotion that we are born with. The other negative emotions like anger, sadness, and guilt are acquired in the course of life. We need to process each of them but most importantly, we need to address fear as it is the most basic and deep-rooted of all the emotions.

The moment the baby is taken out of the womb, it is subjected to a whole new environment, and it is in total horror and terrific fear of the unknown. That's why cuddling the baby and placing it on the mother's body even before cutting the umbilical cord is the norm now. The sense of security and familiarity the baby feels on the body of its mother puts its first encounter with the universe on a safe landing note of love. Together with the warmth of the mother's bosom, the baby gets its initial lessons of trust and faith in life.

However, if the initial landing of the baby is on a note of panic—a complicated or premature delivery—due to which it is placed in an incubator away from the mother, the infant gets the feeling of insecurity and fear. This basic emotion has enormous effects on the mind and body of the baby. The inputs from the external environment later in life, starting from home, peers, teachers, and friends, can add on to this emotion of fear. This basic emotion then gets projected into every area of his/her life, attracting similar situations of lack and fear.

In most cases, these feelings of inherent fear are converted to anger, resentment and blame which is one ultimate cause of so many divorces, separations and relationship issues. Invariably, these are linked to feelings of guilt and sadness in the long run which makes hell out of the beautiful life you are bestowed with on earth.

So, while searching for self-repair tools and answers to the huge number of problems you are faced with in life, recognising the impact of early childhood experiences on your emotions and thereby the subconscious mind is not only important but is absolutely necessary. Repression and suppression of emotions will only destroy you in every area of existence. To embrace love and heal yourself, you need to release all those negative emotions from your system periodically. In the Heal Your Life® workshops based on the philosophy of Louise L. Hay, we have a wonderful exercise to process emotions, which is given below.

How to Process Emotions

This exercise consists of writing down all your emotions of fear, anger, sadness, and guilt under different headings on a piece of paper and observing which of each of these feelings are projected by you and at whom they are projected. It may be your mother who couldn't give you the emotional loving care you needed, or your father, siblings, teachers, spouse, or anybody in your life. It can even be you who did wrong to yourself or others, keeping you in eternal guilt.

Once you get a clear chart of your emotional burden, get a pillow. You can do this exercise by yourself or with a partner if it is a workshop.

1. Think of each emotion you want to release. Then jump up and down three times and scream the following words at the top of your voice while hitting the pillow: 'Get off my back!'

2. Then sit down and address every single emotion and person you have a negative feeling towards. Say, 'I release you, I let you go, and I am free.' It can be anger, sadness, guilt, or fear. If you are doing the exercise with a partner, he/she can reply with, 'It is perfectly fine to release your emotions. Thank you. I set you free.'

3. Repeat these steps until you are through with all the negative emotions.

This is a very deep cleansing exercise and should be ideally done in a workshop setting where you have a facilitator to guide you. There are many other exercises, like boxing in the air or with a boxing bag, that help you release negative emotions. I have a client who puts on very loud music in her car and screams at the top of her voice whenever circumstances become overwhelming. This is her way to let out all frustrations and return calm and collected to take on the challenges of life.

vii. Ho'oponopono Technique

Ho'oponopono, which means to repair or correct an error, is a Hawaiian healing technique that allows you to break free of negative thoughts and emotions. The technique, created by Morrnah Simeona and disseminated by Dr Hew Len, is used by millions around the world with profound results.

According to Ho'oponopono philosophy, all the problems that appear in our lives arise out of memories of the past that repeat regularly and must be cleared to bring forth other positive outcomes. It brings us the teaching that we are responsible for everything that happens in our life and that the problem is not in the other but instead lies in us. It tells us that there is some imbalance in us which is contributing to the situation.

It is the amalgamation of all the basic tools we have discussed in the last few paragraphs (gratitude, forgiveness, and love).

How to Practise Ho'oponopono

To practice this technique, think of any specific issue, person, or circumstance in life which you want to change and just say the words below, mentally or out loud.

- I'm sorry
- Forgive me
- I love you
- I am grateful (or thank you)

By consistently practising it, you will release all the memories that are hindering your progress in life. This will bring you back to balance and connect you with your true essence of light and love.

However, to get lasting results, you need to put emotion into the words you say. You need to feel with all your heart and direct the words to those things that are hampering your peace. You need to feel that you are truly forgiving and loving to the people, feelings, and circumstances that are out of harmony in your life. This changes any negative situation for the better. You will create your desired external reality by changing your inner reality.

Lesson 7: Therapeutic Interventions

Not all healing work can be done on your own. Seeking help when you are overwhelmed by life circumstances is nothing to be ashamed of. Many of our problems, when kept to ourselves, enlarge into proportions that go beyond our control.

It is observed that single mothers are more likely to get ill compared to partnered ones. Susan Harkness from the University of Bath says that a Harvard study has confirmed the evidence of increased incidence of health problems in lone parents, on both mental and physical planes. Lack of social support and the stresses of combining work and family may have contributed towards a higher risk of poor health says the study. An alternative hypothesis is that poor mental health among lone mothers may in itself be an important driver of physical health problems in later life. We have seen in the chapter 'Kenzen' how chronic mental stress can affect the body and mind. So, the last tool to heal yourself is to seek the right therapeutic advice and assistance.

Again, there is no one system of medicine or therapy that is universally applicable or appealing to all. You have a plethora of healing systems from every tradition and culture which you may adopt as per your individual needs. It can be modern medicine (allopathy) or any other indigenous systems like Ayurveda, homoeopathy, Siddha, Unani, Japanese, or Chinese medicine. There are also several energy-based therapies like reiki, sujok, acupuncture, acupressure, foot reflexology, magnetic therapy, emotional freedom tapping or eutaptics, etc. to choose from. The name is immaterial. The only factor to be considered while availing any therapy is whether it can radically cure you with minimum side effects in the long run.

I am not an advocate of any system of medicine, nor do I disown any system. I am of the opinion that every system has its own possibilities and limitations, and it is up to you to prudently select the system most befitting your health condition. It is also not necessary that you stick to just one system. An integrative approach may be needed in certain disease conditions. You may have to take medicines belonging to different systems for the same disease as per the intensity and depth of the condition. You may also have to blend medicines with energy healing techniques. For instance, when I was diagnosed with carcinoma-in-situ in my uterus and used to bleed for days on end, I had to take hormonal tablets to arrest my bleeding for the time being. But later I took homoeopathic medicines and did the healing modules with Louise L Hay to finally eradicate the disease.

Having said that I feel that my calling as an author would be incomplete if I don't throw some light on my journey as a homoeopathic physician. Let me reiterate that it is not my intention to coerce my readers into its fold or establish the supremacy of homoeopathy over other systems of medicine. As said earlier, those are purely personal choices. This is just my way of honouring my divine calling. In fact, I believe that no medical system is complete in all respects. I also believe that any medicinal intervention for that matter is just a temporary walking stick as I said to Vydehi. You need to discard it the minute you are free of symptoms and underlying pathology. Further healing has to happen from the inside on a regular basis by making radical changes in your lifestyle, beliefs, and thought processes, thereby eradicating the very tendency to fall ill.

Let me deviate a little from the context to enlighten you about my serendipitous initiation into homoeopathy. Well, I had been adamant about becoming an allopathic physician, in fact a gynaecologist from the moment I learnt to dream, but destiny had other plans. When the results of the medical entrance were announced way back in 1990, my scores were not high enough to get me admission to the MBBS course. The reason I couldn't perform well on the test was because I had been suffering from a severe migraine headache since the seventh grade. However, I was eligible to get into the homoeopathic medical college—my last choice—as it was a system of medicine that was stamped fake, unscientific, and had no social acceptance or dignity whatsoever. I outrightly refused to join the college but my father, a visionary educationist, literally dragged me by the ear and enrolled me for the five-and-a-half-year course, for which I am eternally grateful to him at this point.

I entered my first lecture on the philosophy of homoeopathy with disgust and scepticism but after the one-hour class, I was in love with the basic concepts of the system which promised radical cure of diseases and not just a temporary treatment or management. My professor said, 'If you are after fame and money, you are at the wrong place. But if you are after the satisfaction of being a torchbearer of a true healing art and service to humanity, if you want to go to sleep at night with the gratification that you have given the best and permanent cure to your patient with nil side effects, you are in the right place. Fame and money will come eventually as by-products.' It was absolutely new knowledge to me and resonated with all that I had envisioned as a physician.

I started devouring my lessons with enthusiasm and the next year, when my younger brother bagged the first few ranks of all the medical entrances across the country and got enrolled at one of the most prestigious medical schools, I felt no envy or regret for my decision to follow homoeopathy. But one year later, I contracted a mild seasonal flu. Since I had garnered so much faith in the theory of homoeopathy, I approached one of the teachers in college. She treated me for influenza and in a week, I was admitted to an allopathic hospital with advanced pneumonia. After spending twenty-four days between consciousness and faintness, I recovered under the loving care of my mother and all the wonderful physicians of the hospital. As I staggered out of the hospital premises with not a semblance of energy left in me, I had lost my faith in homoeopathy together with ten pounds and all of my knee-length hair. I was disillusioned, confused, and even ashamed to say that I was a student of homoeopathy. I lost interest in studies and started bunking classes, when a messiah-like teacher joined our college; a young vibrant physician, Dr Ajay Kumar Babu, whose teaching and understanding of homoeopathy came as a breath of fresh air to an entire generation of students. He started demonstrating the possibilities of homoeopathy in every patient that came to the OP and IP departments and I witnessed the miracle of his grace when a sixty-five-year-old lady got completely cured of terminal cervical cancer with six months of treatment. (She was given a timeline of just three months by the regional cancer centre but went on to live for another sixteen years before succumbing to age-related causes of death). I realised then that the system never fails but the torchbearers of the system can fail as it had happened in my case.

Infused with a ray of hope, I personally approached Dr Ajay Kumar Babu with my migraine, still somewhat sceptical but to my utter amazement, he gave me two powders and I never got a headache for a period of six months. I became free of analgesics which I used to gulp five to six a day. When another mild attack presented itself in the seventh month, he gave two more powders, and I have never gotten another attack of migraine till date. It was miraculous! After seven years of shuttling between doctors and different types of medications, I started to live a pain-free life devoid of medicines. I regained my confidence and faith in homoeopathy and totally surrendered myself before this macho man of knowledge. The next three years in college were the best years of my student life. I got to see radical cures for every conceivable disease of the body and mind in his department. 'You name it and sir will cure it' is what we students used to assure every patient that graced our OPDs. From acute conditions like respiratory distress, diarrhoea, and appendicitis to sports injuries and seasonal epidemics to chronic diseases of any name and intensity were all handled by him with ease. Cancer, multiple sclerosis, systemic lupus erythematosus, sickle cell anaemia, rheumatoid arthritis, Addison's disease, Hashimoto's thyroiditis, epilepsy, tumours and cysts of any organ, genetic disorders like cerebral palsy, autism, and psychiatric disorders like manic depressive psychosis, anxiety neurosis, schizophrenia, and obsessive-compulsive disorder are just some of the names that come to mind while recapturing my student days.

From that day in 1993 to this moment, I have been travelling with this incredible teacher of mine. Establishing a homoeopathic hospital, where the principles of homoeopathy would not be compromised, was his dream project which he finally realised with his tenacity and determination. I work as chief medical officer of this sixty-bedded hospital, the first of its kind in our state, with the satisfaction of imparting true and lasting cure to many an ailing soul. With so many living testimonials and paper presentations to our credit, I now stand tall and proclaim that homoeopathy is insurmountable and practically untouched by any number of criticisms or disownment by the modern medical world. Dr Ajay Kumar Babu has shown me, with a lifetime of miraculous cures, that homoeopathy is here to stay as any natural law of the universe.

If you search Wikipedia, you will find phrases and sentences that depict homoeopathy as the most despicable of medical systems. It has been called everything from being a pseudoscience to quackery. My counter questions to all those vile remarks are: Why does homoeopathy loom large as the second most widely used medical system in the world, despite the fact that it is abhorred and dismissed by the modern scientific society? Are people like me and millions of homoeopathic physicians around the world fools to pursue and propagate a harmful or ineffective system of medicine for a whole lifetime? Why do we use it on our own kith and kin, let alone patients? My son, who is now twenty-four years old, has never taken any other medicine till date. Does that mean that he has never fallen ill all his life? My body has been my greatest research lab to substantiate the efficacy of homoeopathy. I have cured myself of cancer and advanced Addison's disease with it. Was all this just a placebo effect? Are my completely recovered patients just mere fanciful imaginations of my mind? Are their clinical and lab evidences just fabricated pieces of paper?

The truth is that the modus operandi of homoeopathy does not conform to existing research protocols. Though there are studies happening in many parts of the world to explain it from the perspectives of nanotechnology, electromagnetic wave theory and quantum physics, no significant conclusion has been ascertained. Yet, the prominence and reach of homoeopathy keep growing exponentially with each passing year.

I close with the hope Galileo had when he was convicted for proclaiming that the earth revolved around the sun whilst the then existing world denied it. Let the truth of homoeopathy emerge from the veils of ambiguity and shine for the wider redemption of humanity. Let's hope that a novel medical community will emerge in the near future that will integrate all systems of healing to impart a true and lasting cure to every disease faced by the world.

'Aude Sapere. Dare to be wise,' said Dr Hahnemann, one of the most visionary physicians of the millennium.

***

With this, we come to the end of the chapter on tools for healing. As I said at the beginning, you may not require all the tools mentioned here. Many of them have similar outcomes. For example, gratitude journaling is just another way of creating positive affirmations. The Ho'oponopono technique is an amalgamation of gratitude, forgiveness, and love. Just remember that to get the best results, you will need to first get familiar with all the exercises and practise them one by one. Some of them can be done in one sitting while others may require more repetitions and consistency.

The next chapter will explain how you can incorporate each of these tools into your daily life.

Chapter 2

KAIZEN

(Change for Good - Baby Steps to a Better You)

In this chapter, I have compiled all the essential points in the form of a shorthand guide to help you embark on your healing journey which I call Kaizen, or taking small steps to change yourself for the better.

Given below is a morning routine that I guarantee will completely transform your life if you are consistent and disciplined.

1. Start every day with at least five minutes of positive energy. Your first thoughts and actions after you wake up in the morning can change your entire day. And if you can change your entire day with consistent positive thoughts then you can change your entire life. Start the day with a prayer of gratitude. Say 'thank you' for the wonderful day ahead. Feel and visualise the magnificent outcomes of the day.

2. When you go to brush your teeth, see yourself in the mirror. Say the affirmations you have learnt to your reflection with lots of faith and positivity. Smile at your reflection and say, 'I love myself exactly as I am. I am willing to change and I trust the universe. I am safe.' You can also use affirmations to set the tone of the day and how you will deal with it. For example, you can

say, 'Today, I decide to live on purpose! Everything that happens today is for my greater good.'

3.   Cleanse yourself and empty your bowels.

4.   Read or listen to some literature or talks that are uplifting; anything that will expand your mind and spirit. You can also read or listen to scriptures or any motivating or calming piece of music.

5.   Perform any ritual—religious or otherwise—you believe in at your sacred space.

6.   Hydrate yourself with any energising liquid. For me, turmeric water with a pinch of pepper and a drop of pure ghee work wonders. Even plain lukewarm water is a good option.

7.   Follow an exercise schedule that includes both physical as well as mental training (For example, meditation).

8.   Have your breakfast with a good blend of carbohydrates, proteins, calcium, and minerals.

Following this routine is sure to give a jump-start to your day.

Now let's look at some tips to keep in mind on your day ahead.

1.   Make it a point to spend some time with nature and the sun every day. Gardening or going out for short walks with your children or pets are some of the options that will do wonders for your mood.

2.   Take time in-between to show your gratitude for everything that happens throughout the day.

3.   Take some time out to stretch and relax in between the daily schedules. This is a great way to rejuvenate your mind and body.

4. Spend quality time with your family. Talk to your children every day. Listen to their views and concerns. No matter what age they are, cuddle them, rummage their hair, establish that physical intimacy.

5. At the end of the day, look back and be grateful for everything. Say your affirmations and express gratitude to close your day.

Long-term Routines

Write down your goals for the week, month, year, and even five years later, in your bedside journal. Affirm and visualise all those goals and see the magic happening day by day. Strike off whichever goals get manifested and add new goals when needed. Get off the daily routines once in a while. Enjoy weekends exclusively with your children and friends. Go out on holiday breaks or dine out. Plan holidays with friends or your children at least once a year.

Regarding Other Exercises

Inner child analysis is best done with a facilitator. If you are doing it alone, be prepared for the emotional reactions that can surface and once you let go of your inner child, do not repeat the exercise. Once the past has been processed, you need to learn to let it go and live in the present moment. The forgiveness exercise and emotional release exercise can be done periodically to wash off any pent-up negative emotions; once or twice a month will suffice. Very frequent repetition is not advised as these exercises will take you into your painful memories each time and dwelling there for a long period is not healthy. Gratitude journaling and the Ho'oponopono technique can be done as frequently as you deem appropriate.

Any change in habits and behaviour requires time. My dear reader, please do not get disheartened if you don't get results the first time you try any of the tools and techniques outlined along the length and breadth of this book. Be consistent and diligent in your practise. Take one small step at a time. You may stumble in between but do persevere with renewed faith as a baby does while learning to walk. Take those baby steps to witness a better version of yourself in the end.

Finally, I quote from the words of my metaphysical teacher Louise L. Hay, which consolidates all that I have tried to convey in the last few pages.

'Loving yourself is the most important kind of love. We all need to be very clear that the love in our lives begins with us.'

Epilogue

(Tryst with Destiny - A Near-death Experience)

It was a busy day as usual at our outstation clinic. As part of my job, I used to travel the second weekend of every month to see patients at our outstation homoeopathic clinic situated 250 km away from our mother institution. Our medical team would camp at the clinic for the two days where the number of patients would be between 300 to 350. Naturally, all of us physicians and paramedical staff would be completely drained by evening. To unwind and replenish after all the exertion, we would go out to dinner on Sundays before returning home.

That day, we had decided on a small local food joint famous for its signature chicken fry. We were famished and the mouthwatering aroma that wafted through the air only made us all the more impatient and when the first plate of the delicious dish arrived, we scampered like little children to get a piece (the little joys of being in a profession you love with colleagues of your own wavelength). I succeeded in procuring the best piece and greedily dug into the juicy flesh. The fun and frolic had just begun when I suddenly felt a piercing, sharp pain in my throat. A piece of bone had got stuck somewhere inside. I impulsively clutched my neck and tried to catch people's attention above all the noise in that dingy restaurant. I frantically gestured with my hands for help as I couldn't move my lips. After what seemed like a lifetime, people took notice. Amongst the shocked faces, the first one to jump to action was my junior physician. She forced me to drink a glass of water. The waiter panicked and gave me a banana (a grandma's remedy) which I gulped despite the agonising pain. Another junior physician tried the Heimlich manoeuver (the technique to dislodge stuck foreign bodies). My eyes welled up and my bladder burst. I felt embarrassed as my clothes and chair got soaked with urine. All hell had broken loose.

In the drama that ensued, I soon found myself at a local hospital but it being a Sunday night, there were no surgeons on duty. The sole resident physician tried to depress my tongue to get a view of the throat. The bone dislodged and travelled further down which only augmented my agony. I wet my clothes all over again, but this time, I felt no embarrassment. The young physician panicked and gave up. We went to three more hospitals that night but there were no surgeons on call anywhere. Finally, it took all the good offices of my sir, Dr Ajay Kumar Babu, and my brother, Dr Hafiz Ibrahim, to pull some strings and arrange for an emergency surgery at one of the most reputed multispecialty hospitals in the district.

By then, I was on a downward spiral, breathless and gasping for air. In the pre-operative ward, a junior surgeon showed me the position of the stuck bone on the scans; it was on the cricoid cartilage, next to the vocal cord. She quickly explained the procedure of the endoscopic surgery that would be done in a few minutes. The staff nurse then wheeled me into the operation theatre and asked me to lie down on the surgical table but I couldn't tilt my neck backwards due to the critical position of the bone. The kind nurse helped me into a comfortable sitting position and went out to inform the surgical team, leaving me alone in the theatre for a few minutes. My eyes soaked in the disinfected room and all the surgical instruments which would be used on me in a short while. A shudder went up my spine awakening me to three possibilities: I may come out like nothing ever happened, I may come out with permanently damaged vocal cords, or I may simply never come out of the surgery. Just the previous week, a similar case had occurred in a nearby mall where a lady had collapsed and died on the surgical table.

This was a moment of satori! 'Haseena, these could be the last moments of your life on earth. Are you frightened?' I asked myself. Faces flashed across my mind; of my son who would be orphaned, my bedridden parents who were dependent on me, my supportive siblings and their families who always stood by me through the worst phases of my life, and my sir, who has been my mentor in both professional and personal lives. I asked myself if I wanted to see any of them for just one more time. The answer came as a calm no! Did I regret any of my life's decisions? Did I fear death and the unknown realms after that? The answer was again a calm but emphatic no.

Right then, I experienced the true meaning of the word 'serenity'. It was the most beautiful moment of my entire life. I smiled inwardly and wondered why this ultimate truth called death is such a frightening prospect for all. I had read stories of near-death experiences where people had beautiful encounters. However, they were all comatose people, transitioning through to another realm of existence and back. Here I was fully conscious and aware of everything around me. As a physician, I have witnessed many of my terminally-ill patients wailing and wishing for a few more years on earth. To my amazement, I felt no such yearning. I made myself comfortable on the cot with a chant from the Holy Quran on my lips. I felt immensely grateful for every moment spent on earth till date. Death seemed like just a transition and not an end to anything. There was a profound realisation that all loved ones are on the other side waiting to get reunited in the eternal tapestry of the universe. It was like a call to that goal of lasting peace and joy, the promised land talked about in every spiritual literature. I was ever ready for my transition.

As the anaesthetist closed in on my face, I promised myself that if I were to open my eyes to this world again, I would write about this beautiful tryst with death.

***

The next day on the return journey with my colleagues, I wondered, 'Why am I being granted this extension of life?' Somewhere as I fell into a deep slumber after the exhaustion of the last few hours, I found my answer. This second chance at life was a calling for something more; to leave a message, a footprint before the final adieu. But alas, the ways of human nature are hard to mend! The momentous insight faded away as I returned to the mundane routines of daily life.

However, when destiny decides to unveil your true purpose, there is no stopping it. Days gave way to months and life took many tumultuous trajectories, both at the personal and professional fronts, leaving their indelible marks on my physique and psyche. Then came the next epiphany in the form of Addison's disease. I started falling unconscious at the most inappropriate of places, including in front of my patients and on public roads. Thorough investigations revealed that my adrenal glands refused to produce any more cortisol. They had decided to rebel against the relentless stress they were forced to bear for years on end due to my haphazard lifestyle. I was a workaholic with literally no systematic regimen in life. The consultant physician at the hospital where I was admitted for investigations advised lifelong steroids to maintain my cortisol level. But I refused to let myself get injected with synthetic steroids to remain alive like a vegetable. I got confined to the four walls of my house for the next nine months, unable to take in any more strain or stress or even brew my own morning cup of tea. I knew there was a way out but even with all the tools for healing at my disposal, I was blindfolded at the time by the avalanche of all the harrowing happenings around.

It was at this point that I incidentally came across an interview of my all-time favourite icon, Ms Sushmita Sen, in which she talked about her fight with Addison's disease. This was like a godsent message. Her beautiful depiction of how she miraculously cured herself with nunchaku meditation and workouts was a wake-up call.

I became an ardent follower of Ms Sushmita from the moment she was crowned Miss Universe in 1994. I would watch all her films and extremely candid interviews. The courage she has shown to fight with the very roots of the Indian judiciary to become a single mother of two adopted girls was even more fascinating and I used to take immense inspiration from her in my journey as a single mom. My respect and admiration for this incredible human being have only grown through the years.

After seeing that particular interview, something clicked within me. I staggered into my office, rummaged through all the homoeopathic textbooks on the shelves, analysed my symptoms, and came up with a medicine (Lachesis) that had not occurred till then. I immediately took those two doses of Lachesis and in a matter of two weeks, my cortisol levels were normal. I dragged myself out of bed, rejoined my gym and yoga classes, revamped my diet, and started doing my affirmations just as I had done fifteen years ago when I was diagnosed with the initial stage of cancer of the uterus. While it was my teacher, Dr Ajay Kumar Babu, who had redeemed me with his miraculous homoeopathic prescription during that crisis, this time, it was my adorable idol, Sushmita Sen, who came as a goddess to reawaken me to the reality that 'come what may, you are the master of your destiny'.

In the next few months, I gave my postgraduation exams in clinical nutrition which had been pending for a long time, got my yoga certification, and went for an international certification as a Heal Your Life teacher. My cup of knowledge was being filled with each epiphany in life. I then realised that it was high time I penned down the insights from all the wonderful experiences life had put me through. My trysts with cancer, death, Addison's disease, single motherhood, and all the trials in my personal and professional life were the beautifully-mended scars of my life. If I were to die without sharing the insights and learnings from all these experiences, it would be a criminal offence in itself.

However, I did not know how to encapsulate all that I wanted to share into the parameters of a book as I didn't have any experience in the field. Should I write about homoeopathy, should I write about clinical nutrition or energy healing or psychology, or should I write about my own journey? I was extremely confused and was unable to decide the way forward. However, during the Covid-19 lockdown, things started rolling like a pre-planned sequence of events. Everything fell into place and I embarked upon this next coveted journey. An author-mentor, Jyotsna Ramachandran, appeared on my Facebook account and guided me at each step to bring forth the message I wanted to deliver to the world. In a matter of three months, my twenty-five-year-old dream became a reality and the manuscript was complete. Through this whole process, I realised that once your intentions are clear and your motives are driven by integrity and passion, no limitations can deter you from the path you are ordained to follow.

Once I had completed the manuscript, I was again at a loss as to whom to approach for the foreword. As usual, I went to my altar and asked for guidance from the universe. There was not even a minute's delay and the beautiful face of Ms Sushmita Sen flashed across my eyes like a thousand suns. I didn't hesitate one moment and just started frantically searching for her contact. After much effort, I got her mail id on which I posted my story and request. Let me tell you, I still don't know how to express my joy when her manager, Ms Neelam Bedichandani, called to say that Ms Sushmita had agreed to my request. After the call, I was literally jumping all around the house like a little girl on her first visit to Disneyland.

I take this opportunity to bow in gratitude to my idol. I don't think there are many celebrities, like Ms Sushmita Sen, who are so genuine and kind to her fans. The way she connects with each one of us with her sincere heart-to-heart communication is beyond magnanimous.

The next hurdle was to find a publisher. I researched about all modalities of publishing, whether to self-publish or get a traditional publisher. It was a task more gruelling than the whole writing process. Again, I surrendered to the universe at my altar and the name of Hay House publishers came into my preview. After an exchange of a few mails, my manuscript was accepted just like that. I am still in awe of the bounties and blessings the universe has so abundantly bestowed me with.

***

Life has been a series of adventures that subtly led me towards my ultimate purpose in life. Every healing crisis that I witnessed was a call to the next module which I could add to my treasure box of knowledge. With each epiphany that exhorted me to reach out to more and more modalities of healing, I was being moulded to become a holistic healer in the right sense of the word.

An important lesson that I learnt from my life is that in spite of all the knowledge and insights, our buttons do get pushed at times and it is perfectly okay to be vulnerable. You don't need to be a superwoman at all times. You need not be ashamed if you feel lost and uncertain at times. It is perfectly okay to get diseased, depressed, overwhelmed, and even feel defeated sometimes. But it is not okay to succumb to those negative energies for long and lament about the challenges that come forth. You are bestowed with all the tools to heal yourself and emerge like a phoenix bird from your own ashes. Life is so beautiful that it teaches you one small lesson with each hurdle it puts on your path. All you need to do is become a receptive vessel that has the capacity to get kintsugied each time it cracks.

My mentor, Babbu Lakhvinder Gill, from the Heal Your Life® community is a living example of this insight. Healing herself of cancer, systemic lupus erythematosus, depression, and many other issues, even while she was working as a worldwide teachers' mentor, again testifies the fact that 'you are given challenges to show the world that nothing is impossible with the set of healing tools you have acquired. Your duty is to impart it selflessly to the world'. Babbu Gill, at sixty-five years of age, is one of the most youthful, beautiful women I have met.

I extend this book as a tribute to all my teachers in life. Gratitude is the only word that describes what I feel right now. Nothing but gratitude.

To You, My Dear Reader

If my story and the experiences of the women I have shared in this book inspire you to awaken to your magnificent true self, I consider myself a victor.

Dear warrior moms, understand that each of your challenges in life is a wake-up call for you as it was for me. We are all headed for that ultimate truth called death and on this small journey called life, each one of us has been given a mission to complete before that final rest. So, do jerk out of your slumber if you haven't already and leave your signature, no matter how insignificant it might seem to others. You are a perfect, complete being and your purpose is unique and magnificent in itself. We all have a story to tell, a song to sing which is uniquely ours. Please do not die with that unsung song or untold story within you.

Most of all, being a mother, and that too a single one, is your greatest strength. Hold this title as a crown on your head. The word in itself holds the ferociousness of a lioness and the softness of the early morning breeze. You are no less than God with the prowess to be the creator, nurturer, and destroyer all at once. That's why in Hindu mythology, many of the images of the divine are feminine in nature.

You don't even have to give birth to be a mother. You are by very nature the personification of motherhood; you are Mary, you are Yashoda, you are Amina, you are Shakti, all rolled into one. Be thankful to your children for giving you the opportunity to nurture them in this lifetime. Celebrate every living minute of your life journey. Understand that once you realise your true potential, you are insurmountable, undefeatable. Walk your own unique path, the path that's only yours to travel.

I conclude with a line from my favourite Bengali poem by Rabindranath Tagore: '*Jodi tor dak shune keu na ashe, tobe ekla cholo re . . .*' It means: 'Even if nobody responds to your call, don't be disheartened. Be brave and walk your path alone.'

I have responded to my calling and dared to walk my path. Now it is your turn, my dear.

Acknowledgements

*F*irst and foremost, I would like to express my gratitude to all my teachers:

To the greatest teacher, the universal energy I call God.

To my first teachers on earth, my mother, Nabeesa Mammootty, a born healer who taught me what true compassion and love for humanity mean, and my father, Dr K. P. Mammootty, my guiding light who taught by example what it means to be a true human being.

To my mentor in homoeopathy and life lessons, Dr Ajay Kumar Babu, the man who taught me to forgive, love, live, and let live.

To Louise L. Hay, Dr Patricia J. Crane (Ph.D), and Rick Nichols, who taught me and the whole world how to heal through the power of love.

To my mentors at the Heal Your Life® community, Dr G. L. Sampoorna, Lakhvinder Babbu Gill, and Omana Hirantara, all who have moulded me to take forward the legacy of Louise L. Hay and supported me at every crossroad of my journey as an author.

To my mentors at Hay House writer's studio, Reid Tracy, Kelly Notaras, and admin Anna Pettit, who broadened my horizons to an international community of writers.

To my author-mentor, Jyotsna Ramachandran, from Author Success Academy, without whose guidance, this book would have never seen the light of day.

To my teachers from kindergarten to post-graduation. One name that will always stay with me, Shyamala Rajan, who inspired me to take up the profession of a physician.

I am deeply indebted to Ms Sushmita Sen who astounded me with her simplicity and goodwill by agreeing to write the foreword for this debutante author.

I thank my dear friends from all over the world, my buddies from school, college, and colleagues of the Heal Your Life® community worldwide, especially my batchmates whom I rightfully call my soul siblings.

My profound thanks to Abha Iyengar, Mumtaz Shanavaz, Ayesha Fazia, N. V. Kabeer, Sanjeevv Somnath, Anusuya Jayanth, Zameel Ameen, Sreedevi Raghavan, Shahnaz Sherief, Milan Jaleel, and Rehna Nibin. All of you have been instrumental in bringing out the best possible version of this humble attempt.

My love and gratitude to the eight protagonists of this book, who allowed me to share their lives with all of you, and the single moms from different parts of the globe who readily gave me interviews.

Most importantly, thanks to my siblings and their families who have always believed in me and accepted me as their family physician, the greatest validation I can receive as a homoeopath and holistic healer. They have been my greatest cheerleaders and resource persons right from the inception of this book.

I am immensely obliged to all the distinguished personalities who reviewed the book and gave creative suggestions. Dr Patricia J. Crane, P. J. Joshua, V. M. Ibrahim, Colonel. Ashok Choudry, Dr C. S. Chandrika, Zehra Naqvi, Ashna Sen, and Lekshmy Rajeev. I am honoured to have received your invaluable suggestions. Special thanks to Dr Patricia for allowing me to use material from Heal Your Life® modules.

It has been a delight to associate with Hay House publishers. Profound thanks to Mr Ashok Chopra (CEO) and the entire team at Hay House India for their tremendous support and inputs. Words are insufficient to thank my editors Sonali Pawar and Aditya Jarial for their patience and goodwill. Aditya was a one-stop solution to all my problems and handheld me through the entire process from submitting the manuscript to publishing. Had it not been for him, the book would not have shaped into what it is. I also extend my sincere gratitude to the marketing manager, Raghav Khattar, and public relations officer, Rajalakshmi, for their timely guidance.

I cannot conclude this small token of gratitude without remembering my dearest brother N. M. Salim who left us way too early for the heavenly abode, leaving a void nothing can fill. I know he is showering his blessings on his little sister with tears of pride.

RESOURCES

I would like to credit the works of wonderful authors like Louise L. Hay, Dr Patricia J. Crane, Rick Nichols, Paula Horan, Harvey Diamond, Robin Sharma, Paulo Coelho, Rhonda Byrne, Pam Grout, Marci Shimoff, Brian Tracy, Joseph Murphy, Eckhart Tolle, Raphaelle and Michael J. Tamura, Cheryl Richardson, Paramahansa Yogananda, Wayne W. Dyer, Brian Weiss, Shakti Gawain, Dr Deepak Chopra, Collin C. Tipping, Vishen Lakhiani, Chris and Janet Bray Attwood, Aerielle Ford, and John Bradshaw. Also, the holy books like the Quran, the Bhagavad Gita, and the Bible, and teachings and learnings from *A Course in Miracles*, *Organon of Medicine*, and *Homoeopathic Materia Medica*, along with the various online articles and published works of the National Institute of Nutrition, ICMR, and WHO.

HAY HOUSE INDIA

Look within

Join the conversation about latest products, events, exclusive offers, contests, giveaways and more.

f   Hay House India

◉   @HayHouseIndia

🐦   @HayHouseIndia

H   HayHouse.co.in

♥   HealYourLife.com

We'd love to hear from you!